IDENTIFY, ACQUIRE, REPEAT

A Step-by-Step Guide to a Multi-Million Dollar Acquisition Strategy

Jason F. Griffith, CPA, CMA

ISBN: 978-1-4834-7322-2 (sc)
ISBN: 978-1-4834-7321-5 (e)

Library of Congress Control Number: 2017911474

Lulu Publishing Services rev. date: 08/17/2017

FOREWORD

Jason Griffith and I first met at the Entrepreneur's Organization (EO) joint venture with MIT, called the Entrepreneurial Master's Program in 2012. I had heard of and about him, but it was our first opportunity to get to know each other. We shared similar backgrounds given our CPA firms, but more than that we shared a passion for helping our firms, clients, and friends grow thru mergers and acquisitions (M&A). He and I shared many stories of how we had done them ourselves, and helped clients do them. His expertise and sharing in this arena is both broad and deep.

His book provides a step by step guide to identifying and acquiring companies. It goes thru a detailed analysis and provides guidance on a wide range of topics including; how to find, how to fund, how to value, and how to integrate. As he goes thru the book, he shares very specific examples of things he has done himself and things he has advised on. I remember once reading the *Journal of Accountancy* and seeing his ad in the back section in the classifieds, he discusses in the book. I reached out to him and talked to him about it and I thought, now that is a creative idea!

He points out ways that companies and individuals can use his strategies with little to no money down to expand their revenue, profit and cash flow. Jason also provides a wealth of resources throughout the book, with references to many folks he has met and books he has read to be used as additional resources to help entrepreneurs as they read his book.

I have spoken on this topic around the world to thousands of entrepreneurs over the years about how M&A can be beneficial for their business and the resounding response from them is they can see the application, but it is just their need to get over the steps required. Once they embrace the process, I have seen some companies grow almost exponentially through acquisitions.

This book is for anyone looking to grow quicker with a better return on investment and time, than they are getting thru traditional means of sales and marketing. I consider M&A to be the third leg of the growth stool and this book helps outlay a way to put it into action.

John Bly, CPA, CVA, CM&AA, CGMA – Author of *Cracking the Code: An Entrepreneur's Guide to Growing your Business Through Mergers and Acquisitions for Pennies on the Dollar*, CEO of LBA Haynes Strand, PLLC, Managing Director LBA Haynes Strand Capital Advisors. LLC, and EO Global Board of Director

ACKNOWLEDGMENTS

When I was growing up, my parents had a motivational poster hanging in the hall outside my room. The picture on the poster is a photo from an old time gymnasium, with the picture taken from the top of the key on the basketball court. The light is shining in on the court from outside and the rays of the sun are evident. The quote at the bottom says "Opportunity: You always miss 100% of the shots you don't take." This poster is one of the many snippets of positive thinking and motivational thoughts my parents instilled in me as I was growing up. That poster has been hanging there since the early 90's and to this day is still there for my children to see when we go to the house.

First and foremost, I would like to thank my Lord and for the inspiration from the words I read. Reading Proverbs every day with the kids to hear the words of Solomon is amazing. Continuing to seek wisdom each day helps provide each one of us an extra step closer to improvement. "By wisdom a house is built, and by understanding it is established; by knowledge the rooms are filled with all precious and pleasant riches. A wise man is full of strength and a man of knowledge enhances his might, for by wise guidance you can wage your war, and in abundance of counselors there is victory." The words of Solomon in Proverbs 24:4-6 (ESV).

To the many members of Entrepreneurs' Organization (EO) which helped inspire the actions in this book: Your experience sharing, learning, friendship and expertise have all given me knowledge which anyone would be blessed to know. I am grateful for you all.

I would like to thank my parents for always believing in me and encouraging me. Not only in the good times, but in the hard times. To my father, all those times that I was at your office or being inquisitive or the times you had me listen to motivational tapes, I cannot thank you enough for investing that time in me and my development. I strive to be as good a father to my children as you are to me. To my mother, looking down on me from heaven, thank you from the bottom of my heart for always being there. To my brother, despite the fact you still tell fibs to your children and mine about things from when we were kids, I love you greatly and am inspired by all you do.

I would like to thank my daughters. Even though you did not know I was working on this for most of the time, when we would drive to school every day and each set our goals for the day, the "project I am working on" that I would keep mentioning was this book. Thank you for inspiring me with your inquiring nature as, without knowing it, some of the thoughts in here are driven from questions you asked which made me ask the question "why" and then turned that into a "why not". To my precious baby Olivia who will be born around the time this book comes out, I look forward to meeting you and am grateful for the blessing you are already to our family.

Lastly and most important to me after God, I would like to thank my wife for all of her love and support. You have been telling me for years I should write a book and when I finally stated my intention to do so, oh how you held me accountable! While this took longer to do than either of us would have liked, I am proud of the product and grateful to have you in my life. You are my everything. I love you.

In brief I want to thank all of my family and friends and each of you as all of you have helped me in some way (most of the time you didn't know it) to get this book completed. This book would not be what it is without your support. I would not be who I am without your support. Thank you. I am grateful for you all.

Erika Griffith
Jocelyn Griffith
Jolie Griffith
Olivia Griffith

Steven F. Griffith, Sr.
MaryElizabeth Griffith
Steven F. Griffith, Jr.
Wrigley
EO Las Vegas
Mario Stadtlander
Michael Caparso
Rich Scaglione
Theresa Fette
Tom Andrulis
Christopher Roth
Xavier Peterson
Scott McManus
Carrie Carter-Cooper
Scott Fritz
Mike West
Ian McNeil
Mark Brennan
Paul Weinberg
Pepe Charles
Lee Coate
Shane Philip
Murray Conradie
Scot Ross
Tom Miller
Shai Lustgarten
Brent Scalia
Brent Beaulieu
Collin Schuhmacher
Tyler Adkerson
Ford Church
John Diasselliss
Chris Chambers
Brian Axelrad
Royal Alexander
Matthew Schultz

Wendy De La Torre
Swanandi Redkar
Arthur De Joya
Marlene Hutcheson
Chris Whetman
Philip Zhang

And of course my EO EMP Class of 2015:

Brian Brault
Syen Sultan Ahmed
Sid Bala
Ben Baldwin
Natacha Beim
Barney Beukes
Andrew Blickstein
Brandon Blum
John Bly
Kevin Choquette
Blair Christianson
Kathy Colace Laurinaitis
Kevin Conlon
John Dewey
Bill Douglas
Brad Dupee
Hemraj Dhakal
Joaquin Cordero
Patrick Ellis
Cem Erdem
Jane Fraser
Peter Fan
Andy Galbally
David Gatchell
Lynn Harden
Brian Heather
Kristi Herold

Brad Howard
Judy Huang
Suraj Jaising
Aaron Kennard
Michel Kripalani
Govindh Jayaraman
Nico Wyrobek
Dieter Lang
Julia Langkraehr
Eran Lobel
Rory Mccaw
Michael Luckenbaugh
Amber McCrocklin
Sean McDade
Jack McDonald
Thomas McManus
Paul Meester
Andrea Metil
Ryan Mortland
Joao Mucciolo
Gerard Murtagh
Jaime Nolan
Anthony Okoye
Mohammad Ovais
Nina Paulson
Deron Quon
Mose Ramieh III
Marie Seipenko
Pieter Smits
Stefan Stefaniak
Corey Tisdale
Joel Thevoz
Rene Wiertz
Michelle Willette
Randy Woods
Paige Zinn

CONTENTS

PART THREE: REPEAT

CHAPTER 1

Why to Acquire/Timeline/How Do People Normally Do It

WHY TO ACQUIRE, WHAT IS YOUR TIMELINE, AND HOW DO PEOPLE NORMALLY DO IT.

One of my favorite short stories is about a small town outside a major city which had competing fire departments. One was the official fire department and the other was a local volunteer fire department. During a busy weekend, a barn caught fire. It wasn't long before both fire stations got word of the fire. Both of them sounded their alarms, packed up and raced towards the blaze. The volunteer fire department happened to arrive first and was able to put out the fire. Not even one minute after the fire was out, the official fire truck arrived, and the fire chief asked, "What did you do to put out the fire?" The volunteer fire fighter explained the methods that they used. The fire chief got very upset and said, "That's not right, that's not how you put a fire out, you did that wrong!" The volunteer fire fighter just looked at him, smiled, turned and walked away. The volunteer fire fighter recognized that yes, there may be more traditional ways of putting out fires, and maybe even safer ways of doing so, but for the moment, they were pleased with their ability to get the job done.

That story is somewhat of a parable of what this book is about. The methods I discuss here are not traditional, and likely will never make it into a Mergers and Acquisitions text book, or be covered by the *Harvard Business Review*. However, they work.

The methods discussed here are not theoretical, they are from real world experience.

The methods are not for everyone. They won't work for all buyers, and they won't work for all sellers. Abraham Lincoln once said, "You can please all of the people some of time and some of the people all of the time, but you can't please all of the people all of the time." That's what this book is. My intent is not to give you a tell-all, cookie-cutter approach that will work in every case. My goal is to give you a quick way to determine if the situation you are considering will work, and how to create a repeatable process to grow your business through acquisitions.

I use "I" and "we" throughout the book, but I want to be clear, I would not have been able to accomplish all the acquisitions mentioned in this book if it were not for the people I worked with in the process. The Boards of Directors, CFOs or Presidents, and even the administrative departments all played instrumental roles in the process.

WE have used these methods, and in the process have acquired over a dozen businesses with aggregate sales of approximately $100 million in revenue. Many of the acquisitions have been a success, while some have unfortunately failed. We are relating those experiences here to help you acquire a company while at the same time to potentially help you avoid some of the pitfalls we encountered.

This book makes references to other books and Internet resources which have additional information. These are books and companies we have used in the past with good results; we make no representation if you will have the same positive experiences with their products and services that we did.

I met up with a friend of mine recently, and he and I talked about the books we are reading. We joked how we did not feel comfortable saying we had "read" a book if we hadn't finished it. This is NOT one of those books. The layout of this book is probably different from others you have read. You can skip around to different sections, or you can read all the way through from start to finish. There is no right or wrong way to read it.

There are some case studies and examples in the margins, and snippets of information we have accumulated over the years.

Entrepreneurial Masters Program (EMP)

A few years ago I went to an application-only business seminar on the MIT campus hosted by the Entrepreneurs' Organization. The Entrepreneurial Masters Program is a 3-year program for approximately 63 business owners. I had applied once before and didn't make it. On the first day, Brian, our facilitator, or leader as, stood at the front of the room and said, "If you are looking to grow your business by 5 - 10% per year, then this class is not for you. The people in this room are looking to grow at double- or triple-digit rates for the next 3 years. That's why we are here." The program presented many of the ideas you will read in this book, as well as many, many more.

Crystal Ball and Rental Properties

Imagine you find a crystal ball. There is a note on the crystal ball that says it will tell you where you will be able to find real estate deals which will be tremendously profitable. The ball will tell you where you can find rental properties which have had positive cash flow for the last decade, and where the owner is willing to sell for an amount equal to the cash flow from the property so you won't have to take out a mortgage. That would be great.

In this book I will use many comparisons to rental properties. In my coaching and my talks I have found that it is easier for most people to understand buying a fully leased rental property than to understand acquiring a business. The transaction is similar, but the numbers are smaller and there are fewer moving parts. Once you grasp the rental property model, it's easy to extrapolate for business acquisition. The rental income is revenue, the mortgage payment and property taxes are expenses.

Well, I don't have a crystal ball, just data, and in this book I am going to show you how you can use data to get those investments to grow your business.

Why to acquire

What do you consider a good sized customer? $30,000 in revenue per year?

How long does it take you to acquire a customer of that size?

What if you could acquire a competitor in your industry with revenue of 10x that amount - $300,000 per year?

That's our approach. Instead of chasing $30,000 per year customers, we looked for a $300,000 per year sole practitioner (a business with just one owner) who is retiring. We spent the same amount of time acquiring the business, but we achieved the equivalent of 10 businesses worth $30,000 per year. And there's much less risk and more bang for the buck.

Keep in mind though, it is not just about revenue. When you buy another company, you are obtaining their employees (if you want them), their systems (if you want them), their vendor agreements / pricing / discounts, etc. You are likely also increasing your own overhead, so it's not without a need to move slowly and evaluate every decision.

Let's start by looking at the effects on an income statement. In an income statement there are three sections that you as the business owner should focus on.

Revenue
Cost of goods sold
General and administrative expenses

This is the standard Generally Accepted Accounting Principles (GAAP) approach.

Book Reference: *Profit First* **by Mike Michalowicz. This is an easy read and lays out a simple method to get leaps and bounds ahead in your business and personal cash flow. The premise is to flip the standard accounting model on its head, <u>paying yourself first</u> and making more from your business.**

Here are some specific examples, with very simplified math.

Let's say this is your financial statement:

Revenue	100,000
Cost of goods sold	70,000
Gross Profit	30,000
General and admin exp	20,000
Profit	10,000

If you are able to increase the revenue by 1% and decrease your expenses by 1%, what is the result?

Revenue	101,000	(1% higher)
Cost of goods sold	69,300	(1% lower)
Gross Profit	31,700	
General and admin exp	19,800	(1% lower)
Profit	11,900	

So your profit actually increases 19% off of the 1% delta in the other items. ✓

When you do an acquisition, your revenue should have a bump up and, ideally, your cost of goods sold should have a bump down. What is important is that your general and administrative expenses should not have a corresponding increase. There should be additional reduction.

What is not factored into the above is that you should also be able to (1) decrease your receivable days, (2) extend your payables, and, if relevant, (3) adjust your inventory days.

For a thorough analysis of how this can work in your favor, I suggest *Scaling Up* by Verne Harnish, or search for 'Cash Flow Story Scorecard,' available online at www.CashFlowStory.com.

How the process normally works

One Sunday, a little girl sat in the kitchen as her mother prepared a family meal to celebrate great-grandmother's 90th birthday. The little girl watched as mother prepared all the appetizers and finger foods. Then came time for the roast. The mother cut off both ends of the roast, seasoned them, and put the roast in the oven. The little girl, ever inquisitive, said, "Mom, why do you cut off both ends of the roast?" The mother thought for a second and said, "I am not actually sure sweetie. When I was a little girl, your grandmother would make these meals for us, and I would watch her in the kitchen just as you are watching me. When she would make the roast, she would cut off both ends, put seasoning on both ends, and put the roast in the oven. Why don't you go in the living room and ask Grandma why she cooked the roast that way?" The little girl went into the living room and tapped her grandmother on the shoulder and said, "Grammie, Mommy is making a roast and she cut off both ends and put seasoning on them before putting it in the oven. I asked her why, and she said she doesn't know why she cuts off the ends, and said to ask you." The grandmother thought for a second and said, "You know what sweetie, I don't know why either. My mother used to do that. Why don't you go ask great-grandmother why she cut off the ends?" So the little girl goes over to the great grandmother and says in a louder voice, so she can make sure she is heard, "Great-grandma, I have a question. Mommy is making a roast and she cut off the ends before putting it in the oven. I asked her why and she said she doesn't know. So I asked Grammie about it and she said SHE doesn't know either, and she told me to ask you. So why did you cut the ends off of the roast?" The great-grandmother just sat there, had a little chuckle and said, "Why sweetie, I used to cut the ends off because the pan I had was too small to hold the entire roast and it wouldn't fit in the oven if I didn't do that." Moral of the story: just because something was (or is) done in a <u>certain</u> way, does not make it the <u>only</u> way.

First, of course, you have to decide that you want to buy a business. Maybe it is part of your 3 - 5 year plan. Maybe you need to acquire a talent pool to replace people you currently have. Maybe you just want to make more $$ and dominate your industry. We discuss the many positive reasons to acquire businesses throughout the book. But the real fun (or challenge, depending on how you view it) is finding the right company to buy.

You have to do your research and due diligence on the companies you want to buy. ✓

Once you find the one you want to buy, you now have to figure out how to buy them.

How do people normally finance the purchase?

According to the book *"Entrepreneur's How to Buy a Business,"* by *Entrepreneurs* magazine, you can finance an acquisition in these ways:

1. Use the seller's assets: you leverage their assets with a bank loan to buy them out. For example, they have $2 million in inventory and you borrow $1 million from the bank to put down on the business. You then make payments on the balance at set intervals.
2. Buy co-op: you buy the business with someone else. You can afford 60% and someone else wants to buy 40%. I have seen this more with oil leases than with businesses as, in my experience, the person with less than 50% has little to no say. They can go from having an investment worth millions to one worth nothing overnight, and there is nothing they can do about it. (Unfortunately I have been on the less than 50% end of that situation!)
3. Use an Employee Stock Ownership Plan (ESOP). I know professionals who love ESOPs, and I know others who hate them. In this approach the employees of the company buy out the majority ownership. There are many structures to make this work. However, there are a lot more rules and regulations in this approach, and it can backfire just as often as it succeeds as there are many moving parts

4. Lease with an option to buy: you start running the business to prove to your investors / the seller / the bank that you have what it takes to be successful after a purchase. There are risks to this approach, and I would be hard pressed to recommend it to a seller, because if you run it into the ground, they have already given up control. Another option is to purchase a small portion of the interest with the option to buy more over time.

5. Assume liabilities or decline receivables: the business owner might be in a pickle with a personal guarantee on a lease or bank loan, or the business has accumulated so much in liabilities that the owner would be happy just to get that albatross removed.

There are inherent limitations and difficulties to each of the above approaches. Take buying a rental property as an analogy. In its simplest form, a rental property IS a business. It has customers (usually only one unless it is a duplex or apartment complex). It has vendors and possibly creditors (i.e. mortgage). You collect revenue and pay expenses and hopefully have something leftover. For tax purposes you might get depreciation or favorable tax treatment.

Let's say you want to buy a rental property from someone. You can either (1) buy with all cash, (2) get a loan from someone (usually a bank), or (3) get the seller to finance the sale. These are pretty much the only options (I say pretty much as the other ones are more derivatives of the above, just using different vehicles to get the same result). Let's go through each option.

Buy with all cash

If you have the cash and you want a quick closing, or want to avoid bank fees, then this approach might work great for you.

Maybe you want to buy with all cash and then get a line of credit on the property so you can still have 'access' to the funds in case you need them in the future. Maybe the interest rates on equity lines are less than those on mortgages for the purchase of a new investment property.

Maybe you just want to be creative in your estate tax planning. You can buy the house through an LLC and slowly 'gift' units in the LLC to your children with the hopes of avoiding estate tax and/or creditors.

There are dozens of reasons 'why,' and that is just one of the options.

<u>Get a loan (usually from a bank)</u>

This is the typical approach. Usually, the loan is taken out from a bank. I know some people who swear by credit unions as they feel the process is easier (from experience when we bought an office building with a credit a union it was <u>much easier with them</u>!).

Some people borrow the money through real estate investment groups. They willing to pay the higher interest rates as they are planning on combining all the properties into one LLC and then refinancing at a later date. Maybe their leverage ratios are high, or they are betting that the appreciation of the property will be high enough, that it's worth it for them to go that route as the approval time is usually much quicker.

This is the most commonly used option, and there are dozens of reasons 'why.'

<u>Get the seller to finance the sale</u>

I have seen this just a handful of times (with rental properties). One was in 2005. The seller owned thousands of acres, and was parceling off the properties and seller financing them with a 10% interest rates. The market was going through the roof, so he was getting premium prices for the property and a good interest rate as well. For buyers, it was a great way to put a little money down and get into a property quick.

In a seller-financed deal, the seller, likely for tax reasons, will sell the house at a slightly higher than market price and/or market interest rate. The seller serves as your 'bank.' This can sometimes allow them to spread their tax gain over the course of the term of payments instead of taking it all at once.

How do you extrapolate these to buying a business? Well, it's basically the same thing.

Buying with all cash

You can buy a business with all cash, you just need a lot more of it. Coming up with $250,000 for a rental home is a lot. Coming up with 10x or 20x that to buy a business is an entirely different matter.

The limitations of this approach are evident. Just too much cash is needed.

AND even if it weren't too much cash, it is a rare situation that would justify paying 100% up front for a business. There are too many unknowns, and too many representations which you will want to have made by the seller before all of the cash is released.

There are some private equity firms or larger companies for whom it makes sense to just cut a check, without the seller taking any of the risk in the transaction. However, even they use other currency for leverage. They can lock up sellers in long term employment contracts, clawbacks, percentage hold backs, or even personal guarantees on the validity of the customer base.

- Long term employment contracts: I have seen these requiring the seller to work for 5 years after the close of the sale.

ABC's Shark Tank regular Lori Greiner commented to a presenter, "Entrepreneurs are willing to work 80 hours a week for themselves to avoid working 40 hour a week for someone else." That is the case for many business owners and entrepreneurs I know; for them to work for someone else would be torture.

- Clawback provision: the buyer has the ability to take back / recover some of the money already disbursed. If the seller says X, Y and Z will occur, the Clawback provision can state that if only X and Z happen, the seller has to return 20% of the funds. The buyer wants this to be done through escrow, since once the money is with the seller, it is harder to recover.

- Percentage hold backs: a percentage of the purchase price is held in escrow and released to the seller upon achievement of some milestone (maybe sales threshold or sales force retention).

- Personal guarantees: the seller is personally liable for the representations. The buyer knows the funds are flowing to the individual seller, and the individual seller is representing the validity of the customer list and the business. Therefore, the seller must agree to reimburse the buyer if something has been misrepresented.

Get a loan from a bank

This is a great route to go. Most banks want to examine what your business does now, and what it will do post-acquisition. They will want to see that you have experience in the industry. In this case, the strength of the management team becomes almost as important as the cash flow.

No disrespect to the SBA Small Business loan program, but in the last 20+ years, I have known fewer than a dozen businesses which successfully obtained a loan through this program, and they despised the process and wished they had never attempted it. I know from personal experience that the process of applying under this program has always proved to be extraordinarily difficult. Banks love it, as it basically removes their risk (the government guarantees the loan for them). But for the entrepreneur and the investor, I have rarely seen it work out. That being said, an internet search for "are SBA loans good?" yielded almost 7 million articles, so maybe you will have a different experience.

Get the seller to finance the sale

It is likely that 99% of you reading this book want to find out how this can be done for your business.

The other 1% are friends and family members of mine who received this as a Christmas gift. Hi Papa!

In my opinion, seller-financing is the best approach for most people.

Why do you want to acquire another company?

Valuation Reasons:

What is the valuation metric used for your industry? It is likely a sliding scale, meaning larger companies get a larger valuation than smaller ones do. You want to think from the point of view of a future buyer of YOUR company. Your business will be more attractive, and you will prevail in negotiations, if you have $10 million in revenue rather than $2 million in revenue. Yes, I realize there are other intangibles, but the revenue piece is a reality.

Side bar: It doesn't have to be revenue. It can be based on customers, or visitors to your website, or EBITDA. There is some metric rule for your business and industry. Find out what it is.

Suppose companies that do 1 mm - 5 mm get a valuation based on 4x EBITDA (earnings before interest, tax, depreciation and amortization), while ones that do 5mm - 10mm in revenue get a 5x EBITDA. Ok, that is a good reason. If you buy a company which has an extra 2 mm in revenue and you get no increase in EBITDA, your valuation itself has already increased 25%.

Here are some examples of this.

Example 1:

You own XYZ Corp.
$ 5 million revenue

$ 500,000 in EBITDA (10% of revenue)

Current valuation $500,000 * 4 = $2,000,000

Example 2:

You acquire ABC Corp., which does $3 million in revenue and presumes the same 10% EBITDA margin.

Doing this acquisition will bring your total revenue to $8 million.

Now you are:

$8 million revenue
$ 800,000 in EBITDA * 5 = $4,000,000

So you have doubled your value (from $2mm to $4mm) with only a 60% increase in revenue because of the valuation chart for your industry.

Example 3:

Let's presume you have $0 increase in EBITDA from the acquisition:

$ 8 million revenue
$500,000 in EBITDA

Valuation $500,000 * 5 = $2,500,000. This has still increased your total value $500,000 or 25%.

In this scenario there would likely be questions as to why your EBITDA margin is not as high as the industry. The goal is not to buy a lot of revenue without profits, but this is an illustration of how the higher multiple will affect you.

I am not ignoring the fact you have to pay for ABC Corp and their $3 million in revenue. Your deal with them might look something like: $250,000 per year for 6 years, or $1.5 million.

If they went to the market, they would likely get their EBITDA of $300,000 * 4 multiple = $1.2 million.

$1.2 million in the market vs $1.5 million with you

So by teaming up with you they get a higher multiple.

You both win.

Another Example

I had a client involved in a transaction like this. In this regards we were on the receiving end of the offer.

The acquirer knew that in their industry, to get the best multiple, you needed to be over $50 million in revenue. The acquirer was at $20 million and so was my client. The acquirer said:

"Look, we are both at about a 4x multiple of earnings value right now. Combined and adding someone else we will be at an 8x multiple. How about we do this, I will buy you for:

> *4x your EBITDA, paid over 4 years*
> *+ you keep your earnings for the next 2 years*
> *+ we share on the increased multiple when I sell us both"*

The acquirer was an expert and consolidating multiple companies and then selling them to private equity firms. In the above scenario, if he were able to do this, then both parties would win. The acquirer does not really care about getting access to the earnings right now, he just wants to 'rent the revenue' for purposes of shopping it to a larger buyer.

From buyer's point of view: He would move from 4x to 8x multiple

From my client's point of view: He would get a roughly 6x multiple and the buyer would get 2x my clients EBITDA for in essence putting the deal together.

My client gets a higher value than he would currently get otherwise, the acquirer gets a higher value for his business and he gets a fee for bringing my client along for the ride.

WITH NUMBERS:

For the sake of math, let's presume the acquirer was a $1 million EBITDA company and let's presume my client was a $1 million EBITDA company.

Individually they would each get $4 million ($1 million * 4).

At the higher valuation (8x) they would each get $8 million ($1 million * 8). Under the scenario being proposed:

The acquirer gets $1 million * 8 + $1 million * 2 = $10 million

My client will get $4 million up front + profits along the way + $2 million on the bump up in valuation down the road.

This strategy of leveraging multiple businesses for the higher valuation multiple can be very lucrative. It will take a lot of time and convincing, but can definitely be done. In his 2001 book, *How to be a Billionaire: Proven Strategies from the Titans of Wealth*, Marin S. Fridson, discusses many strategies of billionaires over the years. He specially states early on that he will not be discussing Internet billionaires, partly because it was a new phenomenon at the time of writing, but the 'slow and steady wins the race' approach was the focus of his book. One of the billionaire's discussed is H.L. Hunt, a Texas oil tycoon and how he would go out to a farm and ask the farmer to name a price for the drilling rights on his land. He then would hurry to town and offer the drilling rights to an oil driller at a higher price. Once he had both sides in place, he would almost simultaneously buy and sell at the same time. This allowed him to make a profit without risking much if anything, but time. That is what is happening here. You are finding out what a multiple companies will sell their company for and then aggregating them and selling them to a much larger company. You are doing through this acquiring them via leveraging their assets or through getting an option on purchasing their business.

Please do not let the font of the paper fool you, it is much easier said than done and there are a lot of moving parts that have to align to make it work. That does not mean it is impossible, it just means that you have to not give up when you reach adversity or challenges along the way.

How long does the process take for an acquisition?

A brief example of a timeline

Here is an example of the time line you can expect. I have seen it go much faster (i.e. 60 days) and I have seen it drag out for 9 months.

- Month 0: Signed letter of intent
- Month 1: Drafts of agreements and defining who is doing what post-closing; suggest having key people meet
- Month 2: Continued Due Diligence, reviewing processes, verifying financial statements, meet employees, agree on integration time line
- Month 3: Focus on finalizing the branding strategy, FAQ's for buyer employees/seller employees/seller customers, website prepared for switch over and any press releases
- Month 4: Closing/Launch of the two companies

Some other reasons:

If you acquire Net Operating Loss

This is definitely a more complex reason to buy the company, but it happens. If your company is structured with a lot of income and you pay a lot of tax (great problem to have by the way), it might be beneficial to purchase a company which carries a net operating loss (NOL). I could spend 200+ pages on the pros and cons of this, as well as the steps to take to make it work, but suffice to say that this is one of the reasons that companies acquire other businesses.

You and your advisers will want to do extensive research on how Section 382 of the Internal Revenue Code could affect this transaction. There are potential limitations on deductibility, timing, continuity of ownership and other factors in this approach.

<u>Use this as a method to monetize the intangibles of your business.</u>

Have you ever been to a restaurant where the service is horrible, or you look around and see about a dozen things you would do differently? Of course you have. People reading this book ALWAYS see things they would improve. That is why you bought this book. 90% of the time it will drive you crazy, because you know you can do it better. This is not a grass is greener view, this is just reality. The fact you are reading this book means you are thinking about ways to grow your business and expand.

Maybe you have learned from one industry tactics that seem to work, so when you see other companies in the same industry not apply those same tactics, you just scratch your head and wonder why? Some people will make a funny or short joke or rhetorical question on social media about it, but you view it differently in how much it would affect the bottom line of the business if they made a couple different changes.

Once I was in New Orleans for a conference, and met up with my brother and some of his co-workers for lunch. We went to a new restaurant, and it was packed. They had a lunch special where you buy any entrée and get unlimited martinis for 10¢. They called it their "10 cent martini lunch." At first I thought they were losing tons of money on the martinis. Then I realized that the place was packed, and the meals were $5 - $7 more than lunch at most other places would be, and I am pretty sure the vodka they were using was not top shelf. Simple concept, worked like a charm. So when I mentioned this to a client with a restaurant in Las Vegas, he responded as if I had just invented fire. He loved the idea. The point is, you are looking to buy a business into which you can put some quick and simple ideas to improve what they already have in place.

Some immediate "low hanging fruit" is adopting a great KPI metrics dashboard, operating system, or score card approach to running your business. Whether it is from *Traction*, or *Rockefeller Habits*, or even the MAP Management System™, whatever system you adopt should help you run your business more efficiently and effectively, and you should start generating revenue from the process when you apply it to the new business you are buying.

Once you start to look at your administrative team as a revenue source, and they see there are ways for them to generate cash, you will start to see your profits increase dramatically.

Now that you know WHY you want to acquire businesses, let's talk about HOW to identify businesses for purchase.

PART ONE

IDENTIFY

What are you looking for?

In the last chapter we looked at: Why do you want to buy another company? We found there are many reasons to do so. There are also many reasons not to do so. You do not just buy a company for the sake of doing it; you should look at the bigger picture. Where do you want your business to be in a year, three years, or five years? Are acquisitions part of your growth strategy?

When I was in college, I had a work study job at the library. It was often very quiet, with few people checking out books or needing help. When I was not using that time for catching up on homework, I would look at the business opportunities in the back of *USA Today*. I ordered different packages to learn what worked, what didn't work, and what interested me. My parents got me a subscription to *Fortune* magazine, among others. My parents were always pushing me to learn, study, read, and just absorb all the knowledge I could. Every now and then, I was drawn to a set of advertisements for Jay Abraham. Jay is a marketing consultant out of California who has been around since the 1970s. His advertisements would have somewhere between 8 to 20 1-page inserts, describing different business ideas and tools to improve your company. His consulting fees (mind you, this was in the mid-1990s) were in the range of $5,000 - $25,000 per hour. His conferences were well outside of my affordable price range as a college student. I signed up for one of his newsletters, *Business Breakthroughs,* as that was all I could afford. I still have most of them. This was my exposure to what he called the "Parthenon Strategy." The premise, inspired by the Greek Parthenon, was to have multiple pillars of revenue coming into your business. When you identify all of the strategies to grow your business, having an acquisition strategy is usually a great idea.

"Would you tell me, please, which way I ought to go from here?"
"That depends a good deal on where you want to get to."
"I don't much care where —"
"Then it doesn't matter which way you go."

— Lewis Carroll, Alice in Wonderland

So let's dive into WHY people sell their business.

CHAPTER 2

Why Do People Sell?

In any negotiation or debate, it is wise to look at what your opponent will be arguing, or even practice debating from their point of view. In that way, you will get a true understanding of what their position is and how best to respond to it. In her 2016 book *How to Raise an Adult: Break Free of the Overparenting Trap and Prepare Your Kid for Success,* Julie Lythcott-Haims argues that children as young as elementary age should start to practice arguing for the other side of their beliefs. It builds up their ability to negotiate while at the same time they learn how to see things from other peoples' points of view. That is what you need to do in business. This allows you to be prepared for their objections and have an answer to what they are going to say.

My father and brother are attorneys, and when I was young, we would watch *LA Law*. I learned early on that attorneys have long held this as a rule for cross examinations: never ask a question you do not know the answer to already. This is the same for negotiating with sellers. You want to think through every possible question you will get and have an answer ready for them. If possible, you want to be prepared to give a response which explains why their risk is actually a strength for the way you are structuring the deal. We will discuss this more with some specific examples later in the book.

Let us look at it from the seller's perspective.

If you do an internet search for "why do people sell their business," you will get millions of results. Some are titled "7 most common reasons," some are titled "3 reasons you should sell," and some are more direct with "The No. 1 reason people sell."

Some of the reasons are:

All eggs in one basket - the owner wants to diversify their investments and 'take some chips off the table' as they have all of their investments and net worth tied up in this one business.

Business Value - the owner may want to take advantage of a hot market to sell 'now.' Whatever the reason (real estate, technology, medical / health care related), if the owner believes they have a hot market and high price valuation, they may be inclined to 'strike while the iron is hot.' If you had an Internet business during the .com boom, that is when you would have wanted to sell. If you had a large real estate portfolio during the real estate boom, that is when you would have wanted to sell.

Upcoming expenses / change in life – this includes kids going to college, birth of a child, death of a loved one, change in focus, even grandchildren born in another state. Remember, business owners are people, too. Sometimes decisions to sell are based on business or industry factors, and the owner sells when it is most advantageous. But other times the decision to sell is based on other circumstances, which might not be advantageous to the owner. I had a client who had to sell because the climate he lived in was detrimental to his child's health, due to the increase in pollen in the air. He had to move his family, and getting top dollar was not his primary concern. His sales prices was determined by how much he needed to move and start over in a different climate. Business owners have different motivations, and what drives them is not always the same.

Financial pressures / distressed sale - this is related to other items listed here, but sometimes a business owner needs to sell due to financial pressures. $500,000 in 2 years from a sale now could be more valuable than twice that paid over 5 years.

Maybe it is a divorce.

Maybe it is credit card debt.

Maybe they have just been spending so much on entertainment, they have fallen behind on creditors for the business (or personal) and just need to sell to move on and do something else. They might have a good business, but are running it poorly.

Maybe there is a personal situation preventing them from effectively running the company.

I am sure you have been in a restaurant or store that makes you wonder if someone is purposely trying to make the business fail.

We once were acquiring a CPA firm from an owner who wanted to continue to work, but she was not comfortable renewing her office lease with a personal guarantee. The business paid the rent, but personally guaranteeing the lease for another 5 years was beyond the time horizon she was comfortable with given her age, desire to retire within that 5-year time frame, and her grandson starting college in a different state. Selling to us relieved her of that obligation, and she did so joyfully.

Family change - I have seen this a couple times, and when it happens it is a very interesting dynamic. The owner built and grew the company for 10-20 years, and in their mind, the business would always go to their son or daughter to take over and run and grow it for the next generation. However, the expectations of the parent are not always the same as the desires of the child.

A few years ago, I met with the owner of a technology company and his son. The owner was 65 years old and lived in California. He told me that he started in his garage and grew this business for years, and soon his son was going to take over. I asked them, "How far do you live from each other?" I expected them both to live in California. The son said that 6 months earlier he had gotten married and he and his new wife had moved to Texas. The son now came to California once or twice a month to help out with the business. It was completely apparent to me, yet completely oblivious to the owner, that the son was going a different path in life. It was a nice sized business with good profits, but until they recognized what seemed apparent to everyone else, it was pointless to pursue purchasing that business.

Partner disagreements - one owner might want to invest and grow the business while the other wants to stay status quo, or maybe the partners are at different places in their lives. This occurs fairly frequently, and you will want to make sure you understand the reasons for their disagreement (if they will tell you), as well as determining which is side has more validity and if you can work past the risks that come with approach. In product type businesses, this is less of a risk, but in service businesses this tends to be more of a concern.

It's also tricky if the ownership interests are different. On one transaction we were handling, the majority owner was the primary person we worked with for the first few months, and he portrayed the company, and his partner, in a particular way. Then we met the other partner, and got his view of the current and future plans, and we were pleasantly surprised. It turned out that the majority partner was out of touch with the reality of how the business was working, and the minority partner's role was much more important than had been previously explained to us.

Just plain ole' burned out – the owners have put in 80 hour weeks for too long and now they are just ready to relax. The business could be doing great, but they have not had the time, or the ability, to put in an infrastructure to train others to help run things, so they are just ready to move on.

Ready to retire / age - their friends are retiring and traveling the world, or their spouse is pushing for them to retire. I have known people who have said "Ever since I started this business 30 years ago I said I would retire at 60. That happens to occur next July, so I am retiring then." and they stick to it.

Bored - their passion has gone and they want to do something else. This could be a result of some of the other items above, or it could be a result of age. It could be that they never really wanted to go into this business, they just happened to be good at it, it paid the bills and before they knew it they had a full-fledged business they had created.

The Bureau of Labor Statistics says the average Baby Boom worker used to hold 10 different jobs before the age of 48. Here is an excerpt from their study.

A BLS news release published in March 2015 examined the number of jobs that people born in the years 1957 to 1964 held from age 18 to age 48. The title of the report is "Number of Jobs Held, Labor Market Activity, and Earnings Growth among the Youngest Baby Boomers: Results from a Longitudinal Survey." The report is available on the BLS web site at: www.bls.gov/news. release/pdf/nlsoy.pdf.

These younger baby boomers held an average of 11.7 jobs from ages 18 to 48. (In this report, a job is defined as an uninterrupted period of work with a particular employer.) On average, men held 11.8 jobs and women held 11.5 jobs.

From ages 18 to 48, some of these younger baby boomers held more jobs than average and others held fewer jobs. Twenty-seven percent held 15 jobs or more, while 10 percent held zero to four jobs. For additional statistics on the number of jobs held, see the tables at: http://www.bls.gov/nls/79r25jobsbyedu.xlsx .

One limitation of the NLSY79 is that it does not reflect the labor market behavior of people who are not in that particular cohort; that is, people who are older or younger than the baby boomers in the survey or who immigrated to the United States after the survey began in 1979.

Another way to examine job changing is with statistics on workers' tenure with their current employer. Such statistics for all workers age 16 and older are available from the Current Population Survey (CPS). For more information on CPS tenure data, see the web site at www.bls.gov/cps/home.htm.

However according to a 2012 *Forbes* magazine article and a study completed by Future Workplace, ninety-one percent (91%) of Millennials (born between 1977-1997) expect to stay in a job for less than three (3) years. Additionally, they expect the average millennial will have 15 – 20 jobs over the course of their working lives.

Do not think that boredom is just for those who were born more than 50 years ago. Boredom comes in all ages.

Fear - they are not sure they can compete anymore given changes in their industry, such as consolidation, competition, technology, new markets. To stay relevant, they will have to commit and invest more, or put in more hours, and they just do not want to do that.

Loss of key employee(s) - their 'right hand person' has left for one of a dozen reasons, and they just do not have the energy to start over again.

New opportunities – the offer of a dream job, or the ability to move to another town with their family might be too tempting. We bought a company from a gentleman who had an opportunity to open up a retail store in a completely different industry. The new business energized him, so he was willing to hand over the keys for no money down and a longer term payout.

Passive owners - the business will die if they don't step in and start becoming active, so they choose to sell to someone who is 'in' the business. That same janitorial company had passive owners, and we decided to sell it to someone who would roll up their sleeves and become more active. We did not make much money (we lost money, actually), but we just wanted the headache to go away.

Get rid of headache - a business owner might feel more like they own a 'job' rather than own a business. Once that happens, you will be able to hear it in their voice.

When evaluating which type of seller you are talking to, be aware of the seesaw effect between desire and patience. If their desire to get rid of the business is less than their patience in holding out for the 'right' deal, you will never get a deal done.

Case 1: Desire to rid self of issue > holding out for right deal = potential for a deal

Case 2: Desire to rid self of issue < desire to hold out for right deal = move on to the next deal and periodically check back

9 times out of 10, patience will switch the seller from Case 2 to Case 1 over time.

In the same light, holding out for the right deal can become a humbling experience for the seller, so you should respect that it is their business, and they can do with it what they want (good or bad).

I mention earlier about my conversations with a software company over about a 6 month period and the disconnect between the father and son living in different states. Valuation was also an issue here. They felt they were worth about 15-20x their revenue, because someone in the late 1990's had told them that was what they were worth. I am not exaggerating. We were having lunch, in 2014, and the owner pulled out of his jacket a typed letter (type writer, not computer) written to him in the 1980's by an extremely well known, at that time, business titan, about how much he appreciated their business and how good their service was. The owner was still living in the past, and valued his business accordingly.

Their perception of the reality and their value was off, and their patience in waiting for that right deal was much stronger than their desire to move on to something else. The owner was in his late 60's, my conversation with him was almost 3 years prior to me writing this, and when I just checked he still hasn't sold his company. More power to him if he is happy with his decision.

As I mentioned, if the sellers' desire to unload is greater than their patience for the deal, they will do anything to get rid of their business.

**REMINDER: Do not presume logic is at the
forefront of every conversation.**

A Real Estate Analogy for this:

When the rental real estate market in Las Vegas was hot, most everyone you would meet seemed to have 1 or 2 rental properties (which that should have been a red flag then!). A client had just had a vacancy in their rental home. Rents in the area were around $950 - $1,200 per month. The client told me, "I am going to hold out for $1,200 per month for rent. The management company found someone for $1,000 per month, but I am going to wait for the higher rent."

I tried to explain what they were waiting for.

If it took 2 months to lease out the home, the rent for the 10 months after that would be:

2 months vacant = $ 0
10 months * $1,200 = $12,000

If they rented it out now, the rent for that same time frame will be:

12 months * $1,000 = $12,000.

So the question was, did they really believe that they could rent it out within the next 2 months for the higher rate? If they did, then no problem, but what risk were they willing to take? If for some reason it took three months, then their cash in-flow over the same period would be:

3 months vacant = $ 0
9 months * $1,200 = $10,800

Yes they would be able to pat themselves on the back for having achieved the higher rent, but it would also be 13 months until they were 'ahead' on their cash flow.

So the question is, why would someone sell to you YOU.

Determine what you bring to the table. Find your doughnut hole.

What is your doughnut hole?

I will try not to bore you, but in accounting there are a couple concepts you deal with in manufacturing.

> (1) By products, (2) scrap and (3) waste all refer to items generated in the production process that have little or no value.

Waste is something created that has no value and possibly even a cost to get rid of, such as sawdust. There is a Joint cost up to a split off point.

A couple examples are:

1. Dairy farm, milk, cheese, cream, butter, and other dairy products
2. Slaughter house, one cow will produce many different various cuts of beef and even leather, taking step further the parts we don't use could be converted into dog food or animal feed. Mufasa calls it the Circle of Life, Generally accepted accounting principles calls it a "by product".

The point is to identify the split off point when you don't need to move forward. The cost of raising and milking the cow is a joint cost of the dairy operation. Once the milk from the cow goes one way, that operation has its own direct costs. Once the cow is determine to become beef, there are its own direct costs in that business units. Prior to that stage, there were no separate costs at the time.

Scrap is considered left over parts from the raw materials. Metal shavings with minor value. When that scrap is reconfigured to create something else to be sold, it is now a by product.

Imagine a bakery. There used to just be a big piece of dough, cut the hole in it and you have a doughnut. Somewhere along the way someone decided that the doughnut hole could become a product on its own. Historically the "hole" would be thrown back into the mix and folded in with the other dough, to create new doughnuts.

The "hole" was originally scrap that was thrown back into the mix to make more of the same (doughnuts). When it was determined you could make both, now there were two items being made from one original sourcing process.

The thing to realize is items can move from by product to a joint product by resourcing or finding a new way to repurpose the unused time or product.

I definitely could have used the same analogy for the slaughterhouse or for the dairy farm, but I don't think it has the same effect if I called this section "Find your cow hoof" or "Find your butter".

Obviously some people will debate whether the doughnut hole is a by product or if it is a scrap that was repurposed to generate revenue. There is also the scenario in which people create the dough for the sole purposes of making doughnut holes.

While I believe the above speaks for itself, I have always wanted to make a reference to *Seinfeld* in my work so pardon me for the next paragraph.

There was a *Seinfeld* episode where Elaine was at a bookstore with her boss Mr. Littman. He asks her why she is just eating a muffin top and she says "it's the best part, it's crunchy it's explosive, it's where the muffin breaks free from the pan and does it's own thing.....I tell you, that's a million dollar idea right there, just sell the tops!" Her boss then goes and opens up a muffin top store called 'Top of the Muffin To You!'. He ends up not doing well and he comes to her for advice and he has to bring her in as a partner to fix it, she says "here's the problem, you are making just the muffin tops. You've got to make the whole muffin. Then, you pop the top, toss the stump." He asks what to do the stumps and she says give them to a soup kitchen, which of course leads into a much bigger comedic event.

The point is, just making the doughnut holes sometimes loses the effect if you aren't careful. I am not suggesting abandon your business line when you find something new you can do. What I am suggesting is see where there is unused time and space and find a way to monetize it.

So I would ask, what is your doughnut hole?

What are you already doing that someone would pay for?

Andrew Sherman has a great Ted talk (Search: "Harvesting intangible assets") which refers to it as finding your Renoir's in the attic and harvesting intangible assets.

How can you take what you are already doing (or already paying for) and turn it into a profit center?

What is the biggest area of waste in your industry?

Where is your biggest area of waste?

With what resources could you convert that to additional revenue and profit potential?

- Your administrative team could take on more work?
- Your Processes
- You have excess office space
- How you monitor it? *Traction* / KPI / MAP / *Rockefeller Habits*?
- What capacity is your current Administration team working?
- At what capacity is your warehouse running?
- Sure you are busy for 8 hours a day, but does your office/store/parking lot/restaurant sit vacant for the rest of the day or all weekend?
- What does it cost you to acquire a new sales person? And how quickly can you get them making sales? How does that compare with industry average?
- If properly trained, what will the average sales person generate for you in annual Gross Profit?

If you can define out in a couple sentences why someone would sell to you and what makes you different from other buyers, that will bring more stability, security, and comfort in the offer when you are asking a business owner to trust you when you say you will pay them later.

CHAPTER 3

Background on the Market

How is the market for your industry?

Obviously, based on your industry, it depends.

However, the research shows the majority of industries have a vast supply of businesses which are for sale or will be for sale in the near term.

In 2013, the Exit Planning Institute (http://www.exit-planning-institute. org/) completed an extensive study called the "State of Owner Readiness." Researchers spoke with owners of all ages, businesses of all sizes, and asked, among other things, "When are you planning to transition the company?" More than 75% stated, "Within the next 10 years." This represents a transfer of about 4.5 million businesses and over $10 trillion of wealth.

Side Bar: If you are interested in acquiring a business, I encourage you to find your local chapter of EPI and save yourself significant time researching how your specific industry stacks up.

So, what about the market for your industry?

According to U.S. Census Data in 2007, roughly 63% of all business owners are baby-boomers.

There are industries with over 2/3 (67%) baby boomer ownership, and other owners that are relatively young. At one industry event I attended I was the youngest in attendance by far, by about 10 - 15 years. That was a huge red flag to me, and it should be to you, too.

Based on research from *Pew Research Center,* approximately 10,000 baby boomers turn 65 every day, with this trend continuing for the next 19 years. The youngest baby boomers turned 50 in 2015.

In a September 1, 2016 *Forbes* magazine article, *"Truck Driver Shortage Is a Shortage of Imagination,"* author Kevin O'Marah dives right in with his opening sentences: "Google the term 'truck driver shortage' and you'll find an endless string of articles from various local newspapers lamenting the lack of people willing to carry the load in this essential link of the supply chain. In the U.S., the shortfall is estimated at around 50,000 drivers, and age distribution of the 850,000 currently on the road suggests it will get significantly worse in the next five to ten years."

In early September 2016, Wealth-X issued a report titled *"Preparing of Tomorrow: A Report on Family Wealth Transfer."* Wealth-X is one of the leading high net worth market research firms, also offering products and services to their clients. They estimate $3.9 trillion will be transferred to the next generation in the next decade, and that this process has already begun. The main concern they noted in their report was the issue of succession and inheritance, specifically, how to distribute an inheritance among heirs. One of the primary solutions to this issue is the sale of the company. It is rare for 2nd or 3rd generations to run a business these days, so the opportunity (and requirement, in some cases) for them to sell is more prevalent.

A study from the University of North Carolina at Asheville estimates that only 30% of family businesses will survive to the 2nd generation, 12% to the 3rd generation, and 3% to the 4th generation and beyond. There are other studies which show similar results of how difficult it is to transfer businesses down generations. This is another reason this is a GREAT opportunity for you and your business.

Specific Industry Information

If you are industry which requires state licensing, then it is relatively easy for you to determine what the industry as a whole looks like.

Here are some examples from the accounting industry:

A few decades ago, the CPA profession started requiring those applying to become a CPA to have 150 hours of college courses. Most college degrees are in the 120 hour range, so students who wanted to be a CPA had to put in 1 extra year, or 5 years of college, with the last year traditionally in a Master's program. However, looking at the chart, you can see that not many people decided to do that, thus net new members started to decline drastically.

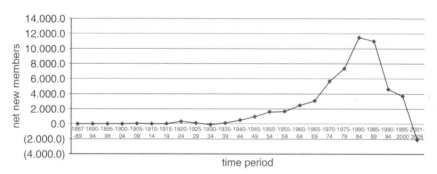

Fig. 1. Net Membership Change in AICPA.

This is great if you are a CPA, as that means more opportunities. But for the market, it is like running out of land. Sooner or later there won't be enough CPAs to service all the needs.

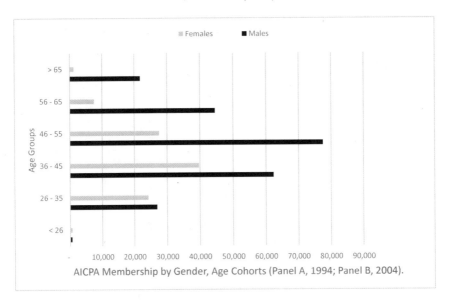

AICPA Membership by Gender, Age Cohorts (Panel A, 1994; Panel B, 2004).

Panel B, 2004

Age Group	Males	Percent of Group	Females	Percent of group	Totals by Group Number	Percent of group	
< 26	582	45.58%	695	54.42%	1,277	0.38%	
26 - 35	26,884	52.57%	24,254	47.43%	51,138	15.28%	
36 - 45	62,301	61.07%	39,712	38.93%	102,013	30.48%	
46 - 55	77,483	73.74%	27,593	26.26%	105,076	31.40%	⌉
56 - 65	44,547	85.61%	7,487	14.39%	52,034	15.55%	├ 53.85%
> 65	21,800	94.38%	1,297	5.62%	23,097	6.90%	⌋
Totals	233,597	69.81%	101,038	30.19%	334,635	100.00%	

Source: For panel A: AICPA Membership Demographics Report (unpublished, dated March 14, 1994); for panel B: AICPA Membership Demographics Report (unpublished, dated July 31, 2004).

This report is from 2004. Add 13 years to the row of 46- to 55-year-olds to bring the report up to 2017, and you will see that every one of them is now over 59 years old. That means that 53.85% of the members of the AICPA are now at retirement age. So you can see that more than 50% of all CPAs are looking to retire in the next 3 - 5 years. That is opportunity. But, that is also a monumental risk for the profession.

How does this help you?

You should determine what industry you want to be in, and what businesses you want to buy.

DO NOT let a lack of experience in a specific industry be a determinant. We have done this in the accounting profession, as well as with a janitorial company, managed services IT firm, HVAC companies, and mobile handheld logistics companies, and I definitely did not have experience in all of those industries when I got into them.

Depending on your background, I would suggest you see if there is an "Exit Planning Institute" Chapter in your city. If so, try to attend their next meeting. These meetings are usually held monthly (the Las Vegas one is a breakfast) and have an educational component. Each month you learn different strategies for exit planning from the point of view of professional advisers (attorneys / accountants / insurance / marketing). I have found the meeting to be a great source of information, and an opportunity to meet with advisers who can point you in the direction of businesses looking to sell.

The Internet is the easiest way to start your search. Or try your local library; you may be amazed at the number of free online resources you can get from the library which do not show up through Google. Search for demographics of owners in [target] industry and see what you find. You can also check out the industry publications for the industry you are interested in.

CHAPTER 4

What Industries Does This Work In?

So the big question is: Will this work in your industry?

From experience, this will work with most industries.

You do not have to have experience in the specific industry; however, if you are already in the same industry, you will have more opportunities.

Much of what you will be doing is along the lines of the adage, "If I help you find $1, will you give me $0.25?" Basically you are saying to the business owner, "If you made $250,000 in profits last year, that's great. Keep it. But if I can help you grow that to $300,000 of profits, can I participate in the $50,000 increase?" On the surface it sounds great. But remember, the business owner is not going to hand the keys over to you after one meeting where you tell him that you can do it.

You also have to remember that the business owner is probably getting at least 3 to 5 sales calls per day, and 10 - 15 emails trying to sell them something, mostly how they can improve their sales leads, close ratio, or marketing. This is actually a benefit to you. This is how you distinguish yourself. You are not asking them to hire you, and you will deliver on what you can say you will do. You are saying that you will work for free to help improve their company and only get paid if you succeed. That is rare, and I would bet they get very few of those calls in a month, much less in a day or week.

Basic psychology says you need to demonstrate credibility and then exhibit vulnerability to build trust. You must do it in that order. In their 2015 book *Friend and Foe*, Maurice Schweitzer, Ph.D., and Adam Galinsky, Ph.D., examine experiments in which a doctor or engineer tried to build confidence via credentials or prior meetings, but it isn't until they showed some fallibility (such as spilling coffee, dropping pencils, or even being a bad karaoke singer) that they were accepted by the subject group.

In his 2016 book *Because of Bethlehem: Love is Born, Hope is Here*, Max Lucado tells the story of Dr. George Harley. In 1926, founded a medical mission among the Mano tribe of Liberia. Over time his practice grew to over 10,000 patients per year. None of the members of the tribe visited his chapel. About 5 years later, Dr. Harley's son died of a disease. Obviously distraught, Dr. Harley was carrying the boy in his coffin to his burial when a local tribesman saw and helped. Dr. Harley broke down in tears on the lowering of his child into the grave. The tribesman ran into the jungle, and told all of the other tribesmen. That night, almost the entire tribe came to visit the Dr. and his wife. The people finally realized he was like them. There was vulnerability and trust. They could see in his face that he was not above them, and he was brought in their eyes to their level. There is nothing wrong with showing some vulnerability in your discussions with the business owner.

Stephen R. Covey, editor of *The 7 Habits of Highly Effective People* and *The Speed of Trust*, is known for his quotes. One of his famous quotes is: "Trust is the glue of life. It is the most essential ingredient in effective communication. It is the foundational principle that holds all relationships."

The point is, if you already are in the industry where you are looking to acquire companies, you are leaps and bounds ahead of someone outside. If anything, you are more likely to understand the nuances, lingo, customers/vendors, sales cycle, etc., and have a shorter learning curve.

Most importantly, the seller needs to know you are not just trying to squeeze their business for money so you can move on to the next deal. Your true purpose, and your personal core values, must be known.

<u>Any business in any industry?</u>

Now, this will not work for all businesses, but it should work for most industries and most businesses in that industry.

A sole practitioner lawyer is going to have a harder time selling his or her law practice than a chain of pizza restaurants (or even one pizza restaurant) would have. That being said, this can be a good opportunity for a lawyer starting out to approach a sole practitioner and address the idea as they are likely not approached that often (if at all).

In real estate, the terms "sellers' market" and "buyers' market" are prevalent.

The definition of these are:

Seller's market - an economic condition in which goods or property or shares are scarce and sellers can keep prices high.

Buyer's market - an economic condition in which goods or property or shares are plentiful and buyers can keep prices down.

Two examples:

If everyone wants to buy a house, and there are not as many available, it is a sellers' market and sellers can charge a higher price.

If everyone wants to sell a house, and there are not many buyers, it is a buyers' market and buyers can offer low prices and has more leverage in negotiations.

In a specific industry, you can have a buyers' and a sellers' market based on the type of business. Typically for service-based businesses, if they are under $750,000 in revenue and/or sole practitioner with not many employees, they are much harder to sell. BUT if you are the buyer, you have more options.

The question most buyers will ask (and you should as well) is how hard will it be to replace the existing owners? Are they really necessary in the day-to-day interaction between employees and management? This is a tricky question. You likely DO NOT want them involved in the day-to-day; it will make it easier for you to replace them when the time comes, and they will be able to focus their time on sales or other areas in which they excel. You DO want them involved to some extent, as, frankly, if they are not involved at all, and they are absentee, their business is likely operating pretty well already and they have a nice steady cash flow coming to them. In this case they might want more for their business, and if they are savvy enough to have created a business like this, they might be less willing to sell unless there is significant cash down.

There are ways to deal with both of these.

<u>If they are active in the business, but want to retire</u>

If that is the case, you would want to work out a 3-year plan:

1st year – same operation as the previous year, just different letterhead. Try not to rock the boat at all.

2nd year – same operation, but you (or another lawyer at your firm, for example) attending meetings and taking part in calls, while the selling lawyer starts to phase out from actual work to more business development (attending mixers or association events, speaking, writing articles, etc.)

3rd year - selling lawyer participates in every other meeting, works from the office only 3 or 4 days a week, slowly phasing out.

This is just an example and every situation is different.

We did an acquisition with a CPA who absolutely loved going to mixers and luncheons. She would go for three hours and try to drum up business the whole time. She loved it. We did an acquisition with another CPA who we would not allow to go to any mixers as he was boring and had no social skills. However, he was extremely smart on technical matters, and could knock out work at a very high level of efficiency, but we had to adapt our 3-year plan to suit his temperament and strengths.

If you are reading this and your company is not ready to be sold (i.e., it would be hard for someone to buy your company and for it to still 'click' the way it does), do not fear. That can be fixed. You should reach out to an exit planning adviser or someone with experience to help you get your company ready for sale. If you do not have a business that you think someone would buy, you do not really have a business, you have a job. Trying to find someone to buy your job is a much longer and harder task than finding someone to buy a business.

A question I receive 100% of the time

I have presented on this subject many times, and the one question I am asked every time is, "Why would someone sell to you for no money down?"

And the answer I always give is: it does not matter why. Business owners are people, too. They get bored with the company. They get a divorce. They hate their partner. Their child is graduating from high school and they promised their spouse years ago that they will sell the company and travel the world as soon as that happens. They get burned out. They want to pursue a new line of work. They reach a magic age at which they have always told themselves they would sell their business (usually 50, 55, 60, or 65). They may not want to sell until Congress changes the tax code, so they will defer their proceeds for years. I have seen business owners with the strangest reasons (in my mind) for wanting to sell, but you know what? It is their business, and they can sell when they want to sell.

It really does not matter why. Yes, you want to figure out why and respect that reason, but each business owner is different. If you talk with a 40-year-old business owner who is aggressive with their growth strategy or views this as a passive investment, they likely will not sell for no money down. They are in the midst of growth and looking for more deals, so they need the cash now vs later. A recurring message I tell people is that all money is not created equal. Same goes for business owners. Not all owners are created equal.

Example:

Sandra is a 40-year-old business owner who sells printers. She started her business eight years ago. She has five full time employees, and works about 30 hours per week. Her business does about $5 million per year in revenue, and puts about $400,000 on the bottom line after expenses. Sandra has a 9-year-old daughter and her husband is an attorney. They take two vacations per year and have been in their home for about 12 years, so they've built up some good equity.

Leo is a 65-year-old business owner who also sells printers. He started his business 23 years ago. He has five full time employees, and works about 30 hours per week. The business does about $5 million per year in revenue and puts about $400,000 on the bottom line after expenses (so, pretty much the same on paper as Sandra's company). Leo's son used to live close by, but moved out of state for work a few years ago. Leo's son (and his grandson) now live about 2 hours away, so Leo only gets to see him on the weekends. The grandson just started playing soccer, and Leo's wife wants to know when Leo is going to sell the company so they can spend more time with their grandson. His home is paid for and he has about $4 million in his 401K.

Given those two virtually identical companies, which one do you think would be more interested in selling for no money down? I think the answer is obvious, Leo would be the one to approach.

It is worth repeating, business owners are people too. They have values and dreams and desires just like you. What you need to find is the intersection between yours and theirs. Imagine a Venn Diagram with the circle on the left being your needs / abilities / desires, and the circle on the right being the seller's needs / abilities / desires. The area where those two circles intersect is where you find common ground and get the deal done.

CHAPTER 5

How to Find Companies to Buy

This is surprisingly one of the easiest steps in the process.

First you need to define what an ideal acquisition looks like.

Actually, FIRST, let's define what the ideal acquisitions does NOT look like.

To me, the ideal acquisition is NOT the company that is running super efficiently with dashboards, scorecards for all employees, mission / vision / values, monthly or quarterly management meetings with key performance metrics defined, etc. Yes that is a great company to buy if you are a private equity firm, but we are buying a company that is not there yet, and we will turn it into that over time. I recently ran across a company like this. I had cold called them to see if they were interested in selling. They said they were just finishing their pitch deck for selling the company and they sent it to me. They were looking for a multiple of 14x EBITDA. All of the benefits and efficiencies were already built into the price of what they were looking for and they were willing to hold out for the right value.

When you buy a company that is performing the best it can in all aspects of their business, it is going to be harder for you to make improvements. You are looking for companies which have some low hanging fruit where you can improve performance. One of the largest acquisitions I put together was for a company doing over $30 million in revenue. The head of sales was a genius. He had been in the industry since I was in high school.

He knew everyone, and everyone knew him. He could tell you within $50,000 where sales would be every quarter for the coming six quarters. He and his partner had built up the company to be a well-oiled machine. However, in getting to know the business and the partners, there were a lot of low hanging fruit available to be tweaked to improve cash flow, profitability, sales, etc. The owners' focus was on doing things the way it had always been done and growing at 5% per year. They had that part nailed down. However, from talking with them and observing how their business operated, there were areas where small improvements would turn in to faster growth, which would benefit everyone. The main tweaks were with items that in other industries were the norm, but in this industry just was not common.

We found this to be true in many of the organizations we considered acquiring, or consulted with about their exit plans. If it's not broken, don't try to fix it. Especially for the more experienced and seasoned owners. I spoke with one gentleman who was in his early 70's, and he knew he was behind the times on marketing, CRM, and technology, but he said at his age he didn't want to rock the boat and jeopardize his income.

What type of CRM system do they have? I looked at four different companies with each having over $15 million a year in revenue, and none of them had a CRM system. One of them had a subscription to Salesforce. com, but no one was using it. They used Excel to track everything. That worked for them. Another did no marketing. I take that back, they had a marketing contract for about $300 per month for a blog, a couple tweets or Facebook posts. That company did over $25 million in revenue. To be clear, these companies were not doing anything wrong (they were making great money for their owners), there were just opportunities for improvement which would benefit everyone. They still had the same administrative team from when they were at $5 million. Again, nothing inherently wrong, but there were so many intangibles at the different levels not being monetized.

The point is, you are not looking for a company that is doing everything right and where you are unable to contribute to help them grow. There is nothing wrong if you want to negotiate or go through the exercise with them. But from experience, companies operating that well have loftier expectations in terms of sales price, cash down, terms, etc. One owner we spoke with was so beyond unrealistic in his expectations of value, when he told me the price, I honestly thought he was joking and we moved on. But then he brought it up again, and I said, "I'm sorry, you were serious with that price?" He said yes, and I told him, "I'm sorry. That's just way out of the ball park and not something we could even consider."

Rule: Don't fall so in love with a deal that you are unable to walk away. There was an entrepreneur we spoke with who I thought would be a GREAT addition to the management team. They had great products, and services that would fit in with ours, and they had a young management team that was hungry for more… BUT, when we got past the initial stages of negotiation, we found out that they had some existing contracts which soured the deal for us. They had some debts with low amounts, but with terms (due dates) that made it impossible for us to continue.

Another example. We were in discussions with a CPA firm which was in perfect alignment with us on everything. Except, the owner also owned his office building, and at the time (2009) the real estate market was at a low, and he would only sell his business if we would take over his building as well. This killed the projections and removed any savings or efficiencies which were built into our financial model (our office was 3 miles away, we did not need or want his building).

Send Out Letters and follow up with a call

For one acquisition, we found the company we purchased the old-fashioned way.

We looked in the Las Vegas publication the *Book of Lists*. Most cities have this. It lists businesses by industry, along with contact information and the name of the owner or manager. The paper copy was free and the electronic version is $39.

We looked up janitorial companies in the area we were targeting. The *Book of Lists* sorts by number of employees, total sales, or some other metric. We scrapped the top four names on the list as we recognized them as large regional companies. We also omitted franchises. After whittling down the list we ended up with 20 companies.

We sent each company a letter, the full text of which is in the case study at the end of this chapter.

We mailed out the letters on a Monday, and by the following week we had two interested parties. We actually had three responses, but the first was just fishing for information on the name of the buyer.

I have used the text of that letter as recently as December 2016, and it continues to get results.

Find the Owner's name

What I do not do is mail a letter to a company addressed to "Owner" and just cross my fingers that it will get there. Once you identify a company, do a business search on your state's Secretary of State website to find the names of the owners. If you are lucky they will have set up the company using their home address. For some industries there is a separate license with the requisite state board (attorney, accountant, contractor, etc.). If you are unable to locate the business on the Secretary of State's website, try the fictitious business license search on your city's website. The goal is to personalize the letter. "Dear Mario" will get you a lot further than "To Whom It May Concern."(The latter may never even make it to their desk!). Once you get a name, look it up on your county assessor website to find a home address. Mail the letter to the home if you can. Do not underestimate the amount of mail the business owner gets at work. If you want to stand out and get their attention when they do not have 100 other things going on, mail it to them at their house. Do not be lazy, do the research. If you want to be successful, take the extra steps to find out this information. It will be extremely helpful.

I had horrible customer service with a top five online bank (if I said the name and you were born before 2000, you would know who they were). I did not receive what I was promised (in writing) in a financial package they were putting together. Yes, I could have hired attorneys and spent money to probably get me nowhere. But instead I found the CFO's home address from his registration with the state board of accountancy at his state's website. I sent him a short letter asking for his help in resolving the situation. In less than a week I had the matter resolved. Do not underestimate the value of sending someone something at home. **Huge caveat to this.** Do not treat their home as an open book to market to them or abuse their privacy. If one letter does not work, do not send another one. In my letter, I apologized for having to send the letter to his house and just asked for him to refer me to someone in the company to help me get the matter resolved. The purpose of the letter was to not resolve the issue, it was to get me talking with someone who could resolve it. The same goes for sending a letter about buying a business. The purpose of the letter is to not close the deal. It is to get them on the phone, that's it. You are offering the business owner something of value to them, so I do not believe it is intrusive to send them one letter at home. But anything after that should go to their office (unless they tell you otherwise).

One thing we have also done before is send it via overnight mail. If a business owner has a stack of mail on his desk, 99 times out of 100, he or she will open up a FedEx envelope before opening something in a regular plain white envelope.

Once the letter has been sent out, follow up with a phone call.

What I do not recommend

What I do not recommend doing is sending one page faxes that say, "Have a business for sale? Call xxx-xxx-xxxx." I get those all the time and they go straight in the trash.

I do not recommend leaving a message with the receptionist saying you are looking to buy the company. That is the seller's private decision and you should not expose the company to the risk of employees getting scared and rumors starting, and it will just come across as a sales call. If you are unable to get to the owner, then ask for their voicemail or email address and contact them directly. If you get the response "I am their voicemail", then say it is a personal matter and try again another time.

Another trick I have heard many times and used many times is call before 8 am or after 5 pm. The 8-5 time frame is when the administrative team is there, but the business owner is likely there before or after business hours and will answer the call themselves.

Find others to send out letters/make introductions

I was hired to help a service-based firm make acquisitions. They were already on track to do $5 million that year, and we had almost completed the acquisition of a $1 million a year company, when the owner said to me, "This is much easier than trying to bring in 20 customers paying $50,000 a year each!"

I asked him to send an email to some of the industry groups he had membership in, to let people know he was looking to make introductions and expand his business through acquisitions. Those letters brought in three strong leads.

We did an Internet search for publications for his industry, and found a handful of them for us to advertise in (see below). I also found a company that does lead generation for his industry.

We contacted the lead generation company and asked for the cost for their mailing list. As expected, they said, "We don't sell our mailing list." I asked with them again, sending the following email:

EMAIL WE SENT:

So the company I'm working with is looking at expanding from current locations in NV and Southern CA.

My initial ask I guess would be if you have any clients in any of those spots or the Salt Lake City, Phoenix, or Reno area, if you would consider sending them something like this? It's purely beneficial to them and shows extra value add for what you are offering to your customers?

Please let me know if you think it's something you can do. You may off the top of your head know of some you just want to make a phone call to about it.

I'm more than happy to speak about it with you next week.

Have a great weekend, thanks!!!!

Jason

Hi _____,

I hope all is well! We were recently contacted by a CPA in Nevada who represents a _____ in that region looking to acquire / joint venture with other firms in your area to reduce duplicative costs, share best practices, and expand offerings.

The firms they are looking for are:

? under $7.5mm in annual revenue range
? roughly 40% product, 60% service revenue
? greater than 30% monthly recurring revenue
? where the owner is looking to either (1) retire, or (2) just stop focusing on the minutia of administrative time and focus on sales or service

Would you have any interest in an introduction to them? We have a strict policy of not selling our customer list or information so if you are not interested, we will not share your name.

Thanks!

The entire process of contacting them and sending the emails took less than 10 minutes. They are the ones who know people in this region who meet the criteria. There was an old slogan for the phone book (for those born after 2000, a phone book was literally a printed list of everyone who had a phone and their phone number, businesses too. Crazy, I know...), the slogan was "let your fingers do the walking." That is what you need to do. Let the people who service these customers do the introductions for you. They are the ones who benefit the most.

In another industry we dealt with, about 80% of the products were bought through three vendors. These were the people who had the most to gain (other than us) from the acquisitions. We said to them "can you introduce us to your customers (our competitors) who have good accounts, in the $1 million - $10 million per year in spend with you, but are slow to pay?" They said, "Of course!" Why wouldn't they? If they have the ability to move those customers into our books, they will get the same revenue with less work. A win win win for everyone (us, the seller, the vendor).

Library/Online research

The Pew Research Center has conducted studies of the number of people who patronize public libraries in the U.S. In 2012, only about 53% of Americans said they had visited a library within the last 12 months, 48% in 2013 and 46% in 2015.

If you get a library card, you have access to their extensive databases for research. Many library resources are more detailed than free services you find on the Internet, unless you are willing to take out a subscription. Your local library probably has over 50 different online research tools that will get you access to information you wouldn't get from a standard Internet search. As an example, one of the many tools is called Mergent Intellect. Here is what they list the description as:

Mergent Intellect

Powered by Hoover's™, Mergent Intellect offers new and existing clients a unique opportunity to access private and public U.S and international business data, industry news, facts and figures, executive contact information, the ability to access industry profiles and much more.

Aside from newspaper archives and genealogical sources, library resources have tremendous information about businesses. Enter the type of business and criteria you are looking for and it pretty much spits out the lists of people you want to contact.

Be creative in your use of the many available online resources. I have used HomeAdvisor.com to find a service based company for acquisition. I started with the ones with the most online reviews as that proved to be a good indicator of how big they were.

Write an e-book or presentation for industry events

This one will require you to do some research (which you should have done already).

Create an e-book on acquisitions in the industry, or the aging population in the industry, and/or about exit planning in the industry. The goal is to create an information source about acquisitions that are happening in the region, and the top things that business owners need to do to prepare. Include quotes like, "When we are looking to acquire a business, this is what we are looking for…"

Same goes for presentation at an industry event. Every industry will have a handful of conferences. Become the exit planning expert about your industry. Contact event organizers and offer to present at conferences. Trust me, I have been to conferences in dozens of industries, all of them are looking for good (and free) speakers, as some of the ones they are paying are really just fillers.

Advertisement

One time we went to an industry publication three days before their print deadline and asked what space they had in the classified section at the back of their magazine.

We agreed to pay $1,100 per month for three months for an ad. They had a section for "Practices for Sale", but we had them agree to create a new category for "Mergers / Acquisitions."

We received a dozen calls based on just that one ad. The revenues of the firms that called were between $1 million and $7 million per year.

The entire contents of the ad were:

_____, a well-established CPA Firm with offices throughout the U.S. seeks to merge with and purchase the practices of sole practitioner and two-Partner CPA Firms.

- Are you tired of incurring the high costs of running a CPA Practice?
- Would you like to work less and make the same or more money?
- Would you like a guaranteed exit strategy from your CPA Practice?
- Would you like the ability to accept engagements without having to "do the work"?
- Would you like to sell your CPA Practice today or name you retirement date?

Contact _____ for a confidential discussion today.

Brokers

I am sure I am going to upset a few people when I say this, but I am personally not a fan of brokers. I have dealt with some business brokers in the past who were great, however, I do not know that they brought much value when we were buying a business. I have used them before when selling a business and the transaction went fine, but as a buyer, I have not seen the value. Keep in mind the businesses we have purchased have required us to deal directly with the business owner selling. That is where we get to find out their true motivation for selling. We also save a tremendous amount of time vs having to run all conversations through the broker. Remember, the business broker more often than not will get paid only when the transaction is done. They are not inclined to negotiate a deal where the seller gets little to no cash out of pocket.

In one case we had reached out to an industry broker and told him, "Our firm is looking to acquire firms with the following criteria, this size and number of employees. We will be looking to creatively finance these acquisitions." The brokers made some calls for us, but nothing real came of it. When I mentioned the way we had purchased other firms, he said "I am not going to be able to find you any one like that, we need to get paid at closing."

Talking with Friends

Find out what you are dealing with and what they have available in terms of their business. I recently had lunch with the owner of a business that does about $750,000 in revenue. After the lunch, I wanted to confirm my facts, and from these I was able to re-create some sample profit and loss statements. I know the industry she is in, including what the employees are paid, what other expenses are, etc.

Paige,

Thanks again for lunch, it was great to finally meet you!

Here are some notes I wrote down after, please let me know if I'm on the right track.

Your firm:

- *About $750,000 in gross sales*
- *50% Service A, 5% Service B, 45% Service C*
- *4 workers + 1 admin + you*
- *After your payroll, the company nets about 12.5%*
- *Rent approx. 4,500 square feet, $1.25 per foot + utilities, about 12 months left on lease*

Your goals:

- *Focus on bringing in new work*
- *High level Service A consulting*
- *Client relationships*
- *Service C work*

*What you **don't** want to do:*

- *Deal with administrative side of the company*
- *Finding new staff*
- *Training*

You would be interested in:

- *Some $ up front*
- *Payments over a couple years on the balance of the buyout*
- *Salary for the work you work on*
- *Commission (for lack of better word) for work you bring in of about 7.5%*
- *Work for about 2 years and then slowly phase out so not working 50 hours a week and on more relaxed schedule.*

After you go through this, please give me a call and we can talk through it or shoot me an email with some of your thoughts.

I have some ideas, but I wanted to make sure I get the facts straight.

For this business, and based on what I learned at lunch, I already have some ideas as to the best way to structure this transaction.

RULE TO REMEMBER: From experience this works best when you look at (1) how can your structure so they get what they want, AND THEN, (2) does this structure get you what you need? If you are truly intending to satisfy the seller and ensure that they are happy with the transaction, then you should be happy as well.

Timing

When you talk acquisition with a potential is just as important as the price.

If you are buying CPA firms, do not reach out to them in December. This is when times are slow, and they are less fatigued, but also when they are about to start their big push of clients (January might be extremely busy) and prime revenue earning season.

If you are buying a company which makes the majority of its money in October / November / December, don't wait until September. They will have spent the entire year preparing for that period, and will be less inclined, and have less time or energy, to be distracted from their business.

Using an analogy, how much attention do you think you would get if negotiating to buy a football team during August - December? If the owners are giving you a lot of attention during their busiest time of the year, that means they are either passive in the business or letting the business suffer while they are talking with you.

Look at your own company. When is the best time for you to make sales decisions? This is not meant to take advantage of the seller, but when they are not stressed, they might overlook why your deal is actually good for both of you. A rising tide raises all boats.

Focusing on ensuring that they get a great deal will help you get a great deal as well, and it will help your negotiation process immensely.

How to keep track of the companies

Remember, as exciting as a deal might be, it is not the only one you will find. There are many other deals out there, so you just have to contact and collect as much data as you can. It is very important that you take good notes. I found two simple ways of keeping track. The first is a basic spreadsheet with columns for the data you collect. The second is a manila folder on your desk with information about each potential acquisition in it. The title of the folder would be "XYZ Company ($10 mm in revenue)" or

"ABC Corp (250 reoccurring customers)" depending on what is important to you.

On the spreadsheet or on the folder, write what is the percent probability. This is a guess, but you should be able to estimate what are the chances a deal will work out. The largest deal I ever did started out at 5%, then moved to 20% after a few more conversations, up to 50%, back to 20%, up to 80%, to 95%. I didn't move it to 100% until after all the documents were signed.

CASE STUDY:

Many years ago, someone I had worked with on an accounting job called to say he wanted to meet. Over lunch he told me about a promotion he had been offered at his work. He was an executive with a large gaming company in Las Vegas. But with this promotion he would have to rid himself of his other business interests. So he needed to sell a company he owned (and he needed to do it quick).

I asked how he originally got into it, and in a long story made short, the prior owner was a friend who had to move for other reasons and, in doing so, sold the business to him.

Now he was wondering if I would take over the business and buy it from him. It was a small company, with revenue of approximately $33,000 per month. He said they would sell the company for $40,000. They just wanted the first $10,000 within the first 90 days and the balance at $1,300 per month, 6.5% interest. This amount was based on the company doing about $2,750 - $4,000 per month profit, so the cash flow from the business would pay for it. But he needed to be relieved of the business ASAP.

I ran the numbers, and given the fact it already had a full time person running the company, it seemed like a great opportunity for acquiring a business. I knew I was not going to retire off this business, but if we could net about $2,500 per month from it, that would be a good start.

A few years later, I decided to sell the company as I had other business interests keeping me occupied and I could not devote the time needed. I spoke with a business broker who got me an offer for $40,000 minus the A/R I was going to keep, so a net of $35,000. I discussed my plans with the company manager, and they said they would buy the company from me, but they did not have the cash to pay for it all up front. We ended up determining to sell the company for $40,000 and they could make payments to me.

You may be wondering, "You sold the company for exactly what you bought it for. How is that good?" But you are just looking at two points in time. You aren't factoring into it the years that the company was making money. I was taking earnings out of the company, and the original $40,000 was financed by the seller. So from a purely cash in vs cash out analysis, it was a completely cash positive transaction.

After I sold it, things were great for a while. Then the business had some challenges, and it became apparent it would be better served if I jumped back in to help them. The company needed cash infusion as well as people focused on sales. My partners and I decided we were willing to give it a try.

We decided the quickest way to grow the top line and not increase our overhead was to acquire another janitorial company. I looked in the *Book of Lists* put out by the local business journal and decided to send a letter to 20 janitorial companies in town.

RE: Letter of Interest

To Whom It May Concern:

My name is Jason Griffith. I am the owner of a local consulting firm in town. One of my clients is a growing janitorial company that would like to expand their business.

My client has approached me to assist with their growth. They are looking to purchase and/or merge with other local janitorial companies in town. If you are interested in selling your business or merging with another company please contact me today.

Please feel free to email me or call me at ###-####.

I look forward to hearing from you.

Best Regards,

Jason F. Griffith, CPA

Out of the 20, 15 companies didn't respond. Another three letters were returned undeliverable / bad address. One I spoke with was just curious what type of multiple / value they could get for their business, but made it clear they were not interested in selling. The last one we spoke with said he was recently approached with an opportunity to shift careers / industries, was tired of running the day to day, and wanted to sell his business. He agreed to self-finance the entire company in exchange for payments of $4,000 per month for a handful of months. The company was currently running at $4,500 per month profit, he was taking out $4,000 per month, so basically he was handing over responsibility of the company to me and our other janitorial company.

For us though, this meant we would be able to consolidate office spaces and save $2,000 per month as we didn't need two offices, warehouses, or double utilities. We would also be able to give our employees more hours and better service the entire city.

I wish I could say this had a happy resolution and that my partners and I made money on it, but that is not what happened. Eventually we had to bring in an active partner, and the three of us ended up selling to him.

LESSON LEARNED: In hindsight, I should have just taken the cash being offered when I could have sold it. But I did learn a valuable lesson about getting security when selling on a note and/or when I am looking to buy a business, and what stop guards I can put in place so the seller will never again have to jump back in and run the business. My partners and I ended up losing on this transaction, no doubt about it, but we learned a lot in the process which helped us in future acquisitions.

CHAPTER 6

How Does the Conversation Go?

Now that you know you want to do an acquisition (or you would not still be reading, much less picked up this book), let's go through how the conversation goes.

I have had conversations with potential acquisition candidates where they are very forthcoming with their financial performance and on the first phone call will tell you their revenue and their EBITDA. (NOTE: The majority of time you will have people reference EBITDA, Earnings Before Interest Taxes Depreciation and Amortization, as this is pretty close to their cash earnings before accounting entries. But, it's not the entire story, so don't fall in love with the EBITDA until you get into the financial statements later.) However, I remember one software company that I had 5 or 6 phone calls and a couple of meetings and a lunch with the seller before he would tell me what his revenue was. He was not originally born and raised in America, and his culture required a lot of time to cultivate the relationship and build up trust. After all was said and done, his revenues were about 10% of what I had heard. He was so close to the vest with his company that outsiders thought he was much larger.

Many people I work only share information with a signed Non-Disclosure Agreement (NDA). That being said, before signing a NDA, I have often asked, "Is it within $1mm - $5mm?" or "over $20mm?" and you'll usually get a range. If I know that it is a high profit industry, I might say, "Oh, that's great. I am sure you are probably putting 5-10% on the bottom line?" This prompts their ego to want to brag and tell me how they are higher than others. 9 times out of 10 they will respond with, "Yes, something like that" or they will want to brag, "Actually, we are higher than the average so we are more than that." That information will usually give you enough to decide if you want to go down the path of signing and NDA, exchanging financial information and initiating negotiations.

If you know the industry, once you know their sales, you or your accountant should be able to extrapolate what the entire business looks like. Your industry may be more driven by (1) the number of sales people, (2) the number of service technicians, or some other metric.

What to discuss with them?

Talk about your own frustrations with your administrative team, and how you were able to address those frustrations using processes you already have in place. Show vulnerability and discuss failures in the past, how you have learned from them, and what you have put in place to make sure it does not happen again. What you are doing here is relating one-on-one with them, business owner to business owner, and saying "I used to have the problems you have, but I don't anymore."

Talk with them about movement in the industry (you will want to present some of the facts you have researched), and how in a few years there will be panic and people selling at below market rates. What you are doing here is basically saying "now is the time to sell."

The overall message of the first couple of conversations is not, "Will you consider selling?" It is, "This is what your life would look like after you sell."

This is sales. You are selling yourself to someone else. You are selling the fact that you are an entrepreneur who recognizes the value of what they have built and you would love to buy / merge them in with you, and have them move to an advisory role with your company. You are selling the fact you do not want them to work 60 hours per week anymore.

Talk about the things they enjoy doing outside of work.

DO NOT pander or stroke their ego with false compliments, you have to be genuine.

The people who own the business you are buying have built up something that has fed families for years. You might not even be in the position you are today if it weren't for the steps and contributions they made in the industry long before you even knew you wanted to be in that industry. Do not disrespect that fact or them without taking note of their accomplishments.

The goal of buying a business with no money down is not to take advantage of business owners who do not have options. The goal is to preserve the cash you have to grow the company faster. You must fully intend to make the transaction work for the seller.

There were a couple acquisitions we did which did not work out as planned, and even after several years, neither party seemed happy about them. In one case we ended up returning their client base and did not enforce any of the break-up fee clauses or non-compete items in the contract. We lost about $100,000 in that transaction. But because we handled it honorably, after the dust settled everyone was on great terms and we even received referrals from them. One of the parties I reconnected with 5 years later and we are working on some joint projects together.

This is a small world and I guarantee the industry you are in is even smaller.

There are two types of acquisitions / mergers you will be dealing with: (1) those of companies you already know, and (2) those you do not know or are just vaguely familiar with the company and/or their owners.

If you already know the owner, it can be as simple as grabbing lunch and starting the conversation. You just tell them what you are up to and that you are looking for acquisition candidates.

I cannot say this enough: the entire acquisition process is a sales project.

You want to frame the discussion so the only logical decision is yes!

Example:

You own XYZ Corp, and you are going to lunch with John, who owns ABC LLC. His business does about $3 million per year in revenue.

A conversation with John can go something like this:

You: Hey, John, how's it going? XYZ Corp. is doing great. We just completed our Painted Picture and the employees love it.

John: What's a painted picture? Sounds like something for the conference room.

You: Our painted picture is a view of our entire company, customers, suppliers, and potential employees about what the future holds for us. I have seen them done with videos, but ours is a newsletter dated three years from now. We include the type of customer we want to have, how big we want to be, how many offices we plan to have, and examples of testimonials we want to receive from customers. One of the pieces our employees love most is the fact we plan to double in size over the next three years, and we also plan to do three or four acquisitions during that time.

John: Three or four acquisitions? I didn't realize you guys had that much cash sitting around?

You: We don't, actually. Our business is set up with the partners getting distributions so our personal financial wealth isn't tied 100% to the success of the business. We take some chips off the table every quarter. As for the acquisitions, we are really looking at companies in the $2 - 5 million range that have owners who don't want to deal with daily administrative tasks and just want to be the visionary or sales person, or go to local industry events and do networking, or even just retire and write a book!

John: That's very interesting. How are you going to pay for these acquisitions if you aren't sitting on a lot of cash? (At this point John is starting to think, "I wonder how this would apply in my situation?")

You: There are a couple ways we've talked about doing this, but it depends on the owner and what he wants to do. If he wants to just sell and move on with his life, that's one way. If he wants to be a part of helping us grow and just doesn't want to deal with the day to day administrative tasks, that's another. If he is looking to retire in the next three – five years and wants to slowly phase out, it's another way.

His next question will likely be about a scenario he is interested in for himself.

Path # 1:

John: So let's say he wants to just sell and move on with his life.

You: There are a couple ways of doing this. We would look at their financial statements and determine what the value of the business is and come up with a reasonable payment term based on metrics on both sides. Meaning the seller would have some responsibility to assist in transition, but we would put in a clause to give them upside when we are able to make money off the deal.

Path # 2:

John: So let's say he wants to be a part of the growth and just doesn't want to deal with the day to day.

You: This gives us a couple options. We have looked at setting up a separate entity called a POD (point of distribution) where XYZ Corp will handle all the work and the seller will get a base salary plus, let's say, 50% of the profits + 50% of the equity in that POD. The goal is for this entity to be a sales machine. We could call it XYZ Nevada 1 Corp with a dba of XYZ Corp. As we would say to the seller, "Our processes should increase your sales to existing customers and generate greater profit per customer. If we implement and XYZ does our part, we want to participate in that profit sharing with you."

John: What do you mean XYZ handles all of the work? I don't get it.

You: For all intent and purposes, XYZ Nevada 1 would sell the project and XYZ Corp would facilitate the delivery of the product / services as well as manage the accounting, administration, collection, and overhead so the selling owner can just focus on sales.

John: What about if you want to sell XYZ in the future? Do they participate?

You: That's the beauty of it. Yes, the seller would participate. Granted, it's not a straight pro-rata at the time, but we will document in the sales contract what the formula would be. For example, if their POD generated 15% of the total revenue of the aggregate corporation, then they would get some portion of the sales price. So it's a partnership, but they still have much of the autonomy they had as a business owner, yet many of the inherent risks and market risks have now shifted from the seller to us at XYZ.

Path # 3:

John: So, let's say he is looking to retire in the next three - five years and wants to slowly phase out.

You: This gives us a couple options. What I mean by that is, we can determine the price for buyout now based on certain metrics. Almost as if it's a customer list acquisition and he gets paid on all revenue from those customers for, let's say, five years. OR, we can set up a new entity (SEE DISCUSSION ABOVE ON SETTING UP THE POD). We would put a buyout term in place, something like in Year One the profit split is 80/20 the sellers way, Year Two it's 50/50, Year Three it's 80/20 our way, and in Year Four he is completely bought out. We can be really flexible in these transactions.

John: What would the seller do?

You: That is honestly to be determined. If they are super social and the type of person who loves going to industry events with the chicken plate lunch, and sitting there for three hours, that is great! If they are more technical and just want to review projects at a high level and not do marketing, we can work with that, too. We will let the selling owner drive much of the conversation about what they will do based on what they are best at doing. We will have a 'decision matrix' put together based on the items they will want to be a part of and the ones that they are entrusting me and my team to handle.

John: That's interesting.

You: Yes, it is. I am super passionate on this, as we have found a way to monetize our administrative department. We have a couple of office managers who have fully implemented many of the processes and we are able to handle so much more bandwidth which will in turn drive more profits to us and the people we partner up with in these deals.

John: Interesting.

You: Yes. Sorry for monopolizing the conversation on this. Tell me about things at ABC LLC, how are things going there? How's your family? Any trips planned?

Try not and have the entire conversation be this discussion. Feel out how the conversation is going. If they are interested, they will drive the conversation and bring you back to the topic and they will always end with "I would love to hear more about this" or "I would love to hear how this applies to our company specifically."

You are NOT trying to sell them on it. <u>The goal of this lunch is not to close the deal</u>. The goal of the lunch is for him to let the idea marinate in his brain, then have a conversation with his wife or business partner about it, and for him to be primed when you bring it up again later. Even if he are not interested for himself, sometime over the next couple months he will run into someone who IS interested and will refer them to you.

SIDE BAR:

So let's say you have the owner on the phone and you tell him it is part of your (or your client's) acquisition strategy to look at companies in the industry for acquisition. Here are some red flags that your conversation will just be a tire kicker and you will likely be wasting your (and their) time.

Flag # 1: What is the budget you are looking to pay for companies? (Or another version of this.) What price range are you looking for in your acquisition plan?

Reason it's a flag: I am personally not sure why that question is relevant. I obviously understand what they are looking to gather from this as to how big of a company you are looking to buy, but a more relevant question would be to ask what size revenue / customer / employees / case load / product sales or some other metric. The 'price' of a company can fluctuate by 20-50% depending on what the terms are. As an analogy, let's say you are buying a home. The seller doesn't say, "So what are you looking to spend on a home?" The terms are what affects the price, which is why most go to a bank to get longer term financing. If you have to pay for it with 50% down or 5% down, that will affect the price you can afford. A monthly payment of $1,500 a month or $3,500 a month will affect the price of the home you can afford.

As I am writing this I received an email back from an owner. I found his company on the internet. I found the owner's name on the "About Us" page, then did a Google search for his name and @companyname.com (his website) and found his email address. (So I would have searched: Steve Jobs @apple.com)

That would have brought up articles or press releases with his name and email address. It does not always work, but more often than not, it does. Well he responded to my email and the entire response was "How much money do you have?". I chuckled as I had just written these red flags and then received that email.

Flag # 2: If they want to talk about anything other than a potential sale price.

Reason it's a flag: Yes, I understand you may discuss the synergies, long term plans, etc., but you have to know if you are in the same ballpark (much less same sport). If in their mind they won't take less than 10x multiple and you wouldn't touch anything over 6x, then no matter how much you both like each other, it is an uphill battle that I don't think either party will win.

"So you're saying there's a chance?!"

To be clear, you may only want to push forward on one out of every five or 10 deals you speak with about this. There is nothing wrong with that. There is also nothing wrong with continuing the conversation if you feel there is a chance for something down the road. Maybe they would be a good joint venture partner or referral source for a different project.

When we were acquiring CPA firms, one of the first ones we spoke with took over a year to get to the point where they were "ready" to sell. We didn't invest too much time into it, but we never cut them off, we just managed our time properly.

As you are going through this process, you will find your own style, conversation, and storytelling ability. It will get more and more comfortable for you.

Recommended Reading: *The Art of Storytelling: Easy Steps to Presenting an Unforgettable Story*, by John D. Walsh. This will help you learn some tricks of the trade for painting a picture for the seller about why selling or merging with you is such a good idea.

CHAPTER 7

Who is the Decision Maker?

During the process of writing this book, my daughter, who was in karate, had just completed her first testing for her next belt. I was digging up old pictures from when her older sister had done karate years before. I searched my computer for 'karate' and found a marketing letter I had sent out about 15 years ago when I was trying to get business. Here is an excerpt from that letter:

Dear Entrepreneur:

Ask yourself, <u>who</u> is the decision maker when it comes to determining if a child will become a new student of yours? I would argue that the child's mother has the final word.

I want you to try something.

Go to a few local hair salons and give them gift certificates to one of your classes. Ask them to give them to their best customers.

Now you've pre-qualified your lead, you have someone else doing your marketing, and if the woman accepts the gift certificate, you've jumped over the highest hurdle.

You may say, "Why should I just give away a class?" Well, you are taking the risk away from your buyer, they have nothing to lose, and if their child enjoys the class, you've got everything to gain!!

In hindsight I see many changes I would have made to the letter (aside from the font), but this was a different time. The basics of it are there, though. The end user of your product or service is not always your decision maker.

I jogged my memory some more, and I remembered reading in a college marketing class about the decision maker. Who is the decision maker for any particular purchase? Well, contrary to my belief at the time, the decision maker isn't always the one who you might think. Much of the reason fast food restaurants with large playgrounds took up so much square footage in the 80's was that the decision maker (the screaming 4-year-old in the back seat) would see it and vote on where to go for lunch.

When buying a business, I have seen the decision maker be any of the following:

- The majority owner
- The majority owner's spouse
- The minority owner, who actually runs the business
- The head of sales
- The CFO
- The Board of Directors
- The CPA or attorney
- The owner's advisers
- Friends of the owner

Everyone above will have some say in the transaction, even if they're not the one who makes the final decision. If it's not the majority owner, you need to become the decision maker's champion for the transaction, the person who tells them, "This is why you need to do this." You have to help them get the owner to agree.

Even if the decision maker isn't the one who officially says 'yes' or signs on the dotted line, you need to train them to 'sell' this great deal to others. The seller-owner must be able to explain the transaction to other people and you won't be there to support them.

We previously talked about the initial conversation and how you are just letting the idea marinate in their mind. The deciding questions will come from the decision maker.

The # 1 question the decision maker will ask the seller will likely be, "How much are they paying you?" Followed by, "How much are you getting up front?"

It does not matter who you are dealing with, everyone knows someone who has sold and didn't get full payment after the first installment, or had their payments re-negotiated after the fact. A good friend of mine, and one of the cleverest CFO's I have worked with, uses the phrase, "You only get one bite at the apple." He always says that you want to get as much as you can up front as you do not know what happens to subsequent payments if they screw up the company.

The decision maker can be swayed if you are able to provide security that the seller, in the future, will receive value greater than what they have at that time.

The hardest part is that the decision maker probably does not know all the reasons the seller wants to sell. If the seller is bored / tired / scared of changes in the industry, there is a strong possibility that they have not shared that with the decision maker as they view it as embarrassing. Trust me, regardless of the business, I have met many entrepreneurs who do not have the vulnerability to be honest about their fears as they feel they have a reputation to maintain.

Bird in the hand worth more than two in a bush

You are selling 'two birds in the bush' over the bird in the hand the business owner currently has. You are asking them to take a risk with a business they have built and worked at for over 5, 10, 20+ years.

You have to make them feel comfortable and secure about the risk they are taking.

71

How do you give them security?

Look at everything you can give. Do not get me wrong, you might weigh all the options and determine that paying them a nominal down payment for a lesser total value works for your business.

We were acquiring a $300,000 total revenue service business. We gave the owner a $40,000 down payment upon acquisition, one of the few I can remember where we gave any cash at closing. We did this as we reduced the overall purchase price by $80,000. For us this was a 2:1 return. The seller had a pending cash need to buy him out of a contract which would have prevented us from buying his business, so if we didn't pay it, the deal would not have happened.

Other intangibles we have given:

- key man life insurance
- removal of personal guarantee on a loan
- removal of personal guarantee on a building lease
- ownership interest in a new joint venture we set up with them.

Use of annuities

An annuity is a product where you put aside money now in return for payments to be made over a longer period of time. There are different types of annuities, but we are only talking about this at a high level. Purchasing an annuity can get you an immediate discount on the purchase price, if the seller will agree to take payments.

If the decision maker is concerned about getting their payments, you can purchase an annuity so the seller has a guarantee by someone other than you.

Here's a specific example.

You purchase a company and owe the seller $10 million. You might be able to leverage the business (based on cash flow or assets) to get a $7.5 million loan. You use that loan to purchase an annuity which will pay the seller $40,000 per month for 20 years. Yes, that requires you to come up with $ now, but you just saved $2.5 million, a 25% discount on your purchase price.

Here's another scenario. You owe $1mm to the seller. Are you able to leverage the business to get a $750,000 loan to buy an annuity under the same terms? Would the seller rather get $4,200 per month for 20 years, guaranteed by a major life insurance company like Nationwide or AIG or Genworth? If they do not need the cash, they might agree to this.

20 years might sound like a lot. It is. But remember, it is very possible that the sellers you are going to deal with are more concerned about security of the money and payment stream than the actual money. They may also have a tax situation which requires them to spread out their payments.

Remember, it's not the price, it's the terms.

I spoke with one gentleman who had a business with revenues in excess of $15 million per year. He told me he was planning on putting 100% of the proceeds from the sale into a trust for his grandchildren. He was in his mid-70s and said he had no use for the money, but did not want to just give away the business. He also said he did NOT want his grandchildren getting a lump sum of cash as he was fearful they would spend it unwisely. Under that scenario, he would actually rather have a secured annuity going to his family vs having to follow up every quarter for a payment and keep his fingers crossed on us getting his payment out.

General concept to remember

One of my favorite things learned in college was multiple regression analysis. If you are not familiar with this, it's a way of using a computer program, like Microsoft Excel, to compare a large number of variables and tell you how they are all related statistically.

The classic example we learned was this. You are debating putting a pool in your back yard. You are listening to all the pros and cons. One person tells you, "It will increase the value of your home by more than it will cost you to install!" Will it? So you start to think. You want to find out if having a pool is a determining factor in the price of a home and if the cost is worth it. You can take data from 100 or 1,000 different home sales in an area and pull specific variables, such as:

Home selling price
Square footage of home
# of bedrooms
# of bathrooms
Pool - yes or no
Age of the home
# of fireplaces
Etc.

You plug the data into a formula which spits out information that can help you determine the value of having (or not having) a pool. The equation, in essence, separates each variable from the other variables to determine the relationship with the end result.

The end result formula could be:

Home sales price = _____* square footage of home + ____* # of bedrooms + _____ * # of bathrooms + 45000*(1 for yes pool and 0 for no pool) - ___* age of home + ___* # of fireplaces

If the above is the formula generated, you would now know that having a pool increases the value of the home by $45,000. So strictly from cost benefit analysis, if you can get the pool installed for less than $45,000, it would be worth it.

The point of this walk down statistics memory lane is that the decision maker (who might also be the owner) is looking at a dozen different variables, some of which you will not be able to see, nor will they ever disclose.

Their selling price or cash at closing may be:

Selling Price = _____ * # of years in business + _____* perceived risk + ___* desire to keep employees on + _____ * immediate cash need for kids college - _____ * plans after sale of business - ___ * state of the industry - _____ * frustration from the business

There could be countless other variables added to the above formula. It is not up to you to figure out all of the variables, but it is up to you to figure out what variables have the highest value in their mind.

You should try to figure out their variables and how you can satisfy their needs. One seller might be indifferent to how long she has been in business, whereas another seller could be locked in on wanting to minimize risk.

Please Note: The formula I just gave is meant for illustration purposes. This is not something a computer formula will tell you. It will be up to you to determine these variables.

Time for you to whip out calculator or excel

If you are buying a business, I would strongly encourage you to meet with a CPA or someone with a finance background who can help you in this process.

Warning though, not all CPAs or people who understand numbers are going to be helpful in this process. Just because your tax preparer knows tax law, does not mean he will be able to help you. Just because your attorney is the best employment attorney you know, does not mean you would hire her to represent you in a contract dispute. The same goes for medicine, the best eye surgeon is not who you want performing heart surgery on you. Yet for some reason, in the majority of acquisitions we have done, the seller presumes that if it involves numbers, their CPA can advise them properly. I have seen many cases where an adviser is just giving bad business advice. From a pure numbers point of view, what they are saying might be correct, but it could be bad business advice if it doesn't recognize the reality of the seller's situation or the business or the industry. They may be making their decision and recommendation from one variable versus the countless variables involved in this process.

Example: Adjusting the variables. It's like turning the knobs to tune a stereo.

We once presented the following to the owner of a service-based company:

- We agree to take 65% of the revenue as our labor cost and to manage the entire business
- You will get a base salary of $75,000 per year.
- We will inject an additional $5,000 per month into marketing (coming from our 65%)
- We will split the profits 50/50 until you receive a total of $xxxxxx
- You only have to work 20 hours per week to achieve the above salary and we will together define the performance metrics

The seller came back and she was adamant that the amount of labor cost be no more than 57.5% and her salary be $100,000.

After running the numbers we were able to figure out that if we changed our offer to remove the marketing we were going to pay for out of our share (and just have it come out of the business), increased her work hours per week to 30, and added a minimum number of new clients per month she had to bring in, it would have the same bottom line effect. The seller was grateful and agreed.

This is not taking advantage of a situation, it is adjusting the variables to get to the point where everyone is happy but with the same end result.

Walk a mile in their shoes

To get to know someone, walk a mile in their shoes. If you do not like what you see, at least you are a mile away and you now have their shoes.

This quote has been attributed to a number of people. From Elvis to Eminem to Kenneth Cole to Jack Handy.

Put yourself in the shoes of the owner of the business you are buying. Really think about their situation. As an exercise, on a sheet of paper list everything you know about them (age, family life, food they eat, exercise habits, how long they have been in business). When actors are researching a role they will play, they go through immense steps to get fully immersed in the role. In preparation for the movie *Taxi Driver*, Robert De Niro obtained a cab license and drove a taxi 15 hour days for a month in New York City so he could become the on-screen master for that role. Now you don't have to go to THAT extreme, but it would not hurt for you to spend a couple hours really thinking about the seller's motivation.

Do you really understand their situation? Do you understand what keeps them up at night?

As with any sales process, what barriers can you break down and what fears can you answer?

Common fears and answer:

> Fear: What happens if we don't pay?
>
> Response: You foreclose and take back the business.
>
> Fear: What happens if the customer base goes down?
>
> Response: That is why we want your help during six months of transition. But you also are representing that the customers are here for the business, and not for you as an individual, so that should not happen.
>
> Fear: What happens if something happens to me, how will my family collect?
>
> Response: We will put a key man life insurance policy in place for you as a secure promissory note.

CHAPTER 8

Due Diligence Process

Due Diligence means many things to many people. Here is the general definition:

Due diligence *is an investigation of a business or person prior to signing a contract, or an act with a certain standard of care.*

It can be a legal obligation, but the term will more commonly apply to voluntary investigations. A common example of due diligence in various industries is the process through which a potential acquirer evaluates a target company or its assets for an acquisition. The theory behind due diligence holds that performing this type of investigation contributes significantly to informed decision making by enhancing the amount and quality of information available to decision makers and by ensuring that this information is systematically used to deliberate in a reflexive manner on the decision at hand and all its costs, benefits, and risks.

Hoskisson, Robert E.; Hitt, Michael A.; Ireland, R. Duane (2004). Competing for Advantage. Mason, OH: South-Western/Thomson Learning. p. 251. ISBN 0-324-27158-1.

Chapman, C. E. (2006). Conducting Due Diligence. Practicing Law Institute, New York, NY.

The practical definition is the same. It is doing your own research into the company you are going to buy to make sure what they tell you is accurate and to find out things that they may not voluntarily tell you.

There are two phases in the process.

The first phase includes initial conversations, when the seller shares with you specifics about their business and their financial performance. This will usually lead to a term sheet or letter of intent. This is not due diligence per se; these conversations will usually lead to the discussion about what will be need to be confirmed during due diligence.

- Did they say they have 24 employees? Let's confirm.
- They said their website has over 1,000 unique views per day. Let's confirm to make sure they aren't paying for those hits.
- The owner mentioned they get 60 day terms with one of their vendors. We need to check their records
- The CFO said they have fewer than 1% instances of bad debt. Let's have our auditor confirm that.

All of the little comments the owner drops here and there are the ones you will want to jot down and confirm later.

The second phases is the actual reviewing of the documents and confirming representations that have been made. What really do they pay in rent? What really is their overhead? What is their true labor cost per hour? What you find and what areas are important to you will determine how deep you want to go. While your initial conversations are based on internal financial statements, projections and conversations, the second phase confirms the numbers from a third party.

In the 1980's, a writer in Russia named Suzanne Massie met with President Ronald Reagan. Speaking on the CNN series *Cold War*, she said she had informed Reagan that, "The Russians like to talk in Proverbs, it would be nice of you to know a few. You are an actor, you can learn them very quickly." Reagan later used this advice when discussing U.S. relations with the Soviet Union. This is where "trust, but verify" came from and this is what you should do. Trust they are telling you the truth, but verify the numbers.

This is what you need to do. You can do this yourself or hire a CPA (Certified Public Accountant) or a CFE (Certified Forensic Examiner) to do it for you. Or you might have people on staff in your accounting department, such as your CFO, who can handle this.

Unfortunately, not everyone is forthcoming. Sometimes people want to sell for reasons they have not indicated and they will do anything to get you to buy them and take that liability off their shoulders.

There are countless ways for people to "cook the books." Here are just a very small handful that you need to lookout for:

1. Not recording all expenses or liabilities in the financial statements.

   - If they don't record the expense, their net income looks higher.
   - If they don't record the liability, their debt looks lower.
   - Maybe they pay a specific vendor or creditor personally. It will make their company look better if they are paying $1,000 per month out of the owner's personal account on a $150,000 debt that they have not disclosed. To find this you will have to look at not just the financial statements for now, but over a period of time. Many professionals recommend 2 – 3 full years of financial statements so you can see the trends. Do they have a large piece of new machinery but there is no apparent liability or cash outflow to pay for it? Keep digging.

NOTE: While you may have the ability to do it, it is almost always better to have someone other than you handle this due diligence as it can tend to create animosity between the seller and the buyer. They may feel you are saying you do not trust them. A third party is required to follow up, so there is an arms-length feel to the research.

2. Accelerating revenues. Just think Enron. They were recording revenues in the current periods for what was expected in the future. Generally

Accepted Accounting Principles (GAAP) state you can recognize revenue when they have been (1) realized or realizable, and (2) are earned (for example when the product or service is completed), regardless of when cash is received.

If a company you are looking to purchase shows $1 million for a sale of a 4 year service contract, but they show the full $1 million in the current year, you need to understand what this means. This means that for the next 4 years, you are required to do the work, but you will receive NO cash from the customer.

That may not be a deal breaker, but you want to make sure you understand it in detail.

I have seen companies debate back and forth with their outside accountant over a revenue recognition item. Management sometimes wants to show the revenue now, but the accountants want them to properly spread it over time.

3. Accelerating expenses. The same goes for expenses as with revenue. Imagine you are looking at company financial statements for the last 3 years.

The owner says in Year 1 they lost $200,000, in Year 2 they made $100,000 and in Year 3 they made $200,000.

That sounds great! What great improvement!

However, look at the details. What if in Year 1 they purchased a 3 year insurance policy for $300,000. They took the expense in Year 1, but it really covered expenses for the periods of Year 2 and Year 3. This was in essence pre-paid insurance. Maybe they did it for a discount, maybe they did it because they had a lot of cash in Year 1 and wanted huge tax deductions because they are cash basis tax payers instead of accrual basis tax payers. The problem with this is it distorts the financial statements.

If you were to fix the 3 year results, you might get something like this:

Year 1

Original Income	($200,000) loss
Add back too much taken	$200,000 (should have only taken 1/3 of the $300,000)
Actual income	- 0 - breakeven

Year 2

Original Income	$100,000 income
Deduct prepaid insurance	(100,000) 1/3 of the $300,000
Actual income	- 0 - breakeven

Year 3

Original Income	$200,000 income
Deduct prepaid insurance	(100,000) 1/3 of the $300,000
Actual income	100,000 income

So in comparison to what you first saw:

Year 1	($200,000) loss
Year 2	100,000 income
Year 3	200,000 income

You now see the results are:

Year 1	- 0 - breakeven
Year 2	- 0 - breakeven
Year 3	100,000 income

Same company, but two vastly different impressions of the management team you are looking to purchase. The revised performance is less impressive as a turnaround.

4. Non-recurring expenses

We were looking to acquire a company and the owner provided financial statements she called "normalized" or "adjusted." We asked what this meant, and she informed us they had taken the liberty of removing the non-recurring expenses or one-time costs so we would see a true picture of the company. At the outset that made sense. But when we got into the details of the numbers in that line item, we found that every year for the past three years there had been 'one time' expenses. If it happens more than once it is by definition NOT a one-time expense. If it happens one time, but it is a cost of doing business or an overhead expense, you should still recognize it as such.

5. Off Balance Sheet Items

Again, this was something Enron used to their benefit (or detriment, depending on which way you look at it).

If you are buying a company that owns a small % interest in a different entity, there is a strong chance that the liabilities of that different entity are not reflected in the financial statements you were given by management.

To be clear, the occurrence of any of the above is not an indication they are trying to trick you, fool you, steal from you or defraud you. It could just be the way they have run their business for years and maybe they presume everyone runs their business that way. In one of my first jobs as CFO, the company had acquired a multi-location business which did not record accrual of payroll or bonuses or commissions. For them it was just the way the industry worked and timing was never an issue as 'it works itself out.' Over time they grew to about 600 employees, so that accrued payroll number being (or not being) recorded could swing the quarterly financial statements from negative to positive earnings. The owners were not trying to hide anything, but they operated their business based on cash in the bank. That is how they operated when it was 15 people and they just continued to operate it that way as it grew.

Background checks

In most cases, the question of background checks comes up. There are many levels of background checks that can be done, but from experience, a lot will depend on how involved that person will be going forward. If one of the owners is more passive in nature and is not going to be working for the company after the transaction, then a full background check of that individual is likely not a primary concern and you can save your money on background check fees. Again, this depends on price, timing, how long you have known them, and what their role will be. For a large acquisition, it is well worth the less than $1,000 to do a full work up on them.

Reps and Warranties

You will want to work with your attorney to determine what "reps and warranties" you want the seller to agree to in the deal. This is basically where all those things they have told you are going on, are confirmed to be going on, and if they are not, there can be repercussions.

For example, they tell you that all the customers are happy and provide a representation of that. Then, once you take over, you realize that you have only half of the customers, and then you find out they have customer complaints 3X the industry average and pending lawsuits from the unhappy customers. In this case you have grounds to go back to the seller. (In this example, this could have been found out during due diligence.)

Your attorney will have their standard reps and warranties they want to include, such as:

- They have the authority to sell the company to you.
- There are no liens against the company they have not disclosed.
- The seller has not granted someone else the right to buy the company.
- Nothing the seller is doing will violate other contracts or agreements.

- The seller owns the stock to sell. (This is important as if they have contributed the stock into the name of a trust, then separate documents / signatures may be required as they personally may not have the authority to sign for the sale).

Most of the reps and warranties will be standard, but your attorney should work with you on specific ones for your situation to cover you.

List of Documents

If you search the Internet for Due Diligence Checklist, you will find endless lists of example checklists.

Basics will be:

Articles of Incorporation (amendments if any)
Bylaws (amendments if any)
Board Minutes
Financial statements
Copies of all leases, contracts, notes payables, agreements
Tax returns for the last 3 years

As mentioned earlier, this level of due diligence is usually done by the accountants and attorneys. This will be everything from looking into pending litigation, outstanding debts and liens, to seeing what type of land mines the company could be sitting on that you will be inheriting. In one case I saw, they literally had interest in land which had land mines they were trying to find!

All of the above is another reason many people prefer to do asset acquisitions as you are less likely to acquire the skeletons in the closet when you do this approach. That is not to say doing asset only acquisitions will be trouble free, but the scope of due diligence becomes limited.

PART TWO

ACQUIRE

There are countless ways to set up your acquisition or merger, driven by the type of entity, the type of transaction being done, and the desired goals of the seller (and buyer).

Traditionally, acquisitions have been one party acquiring ownership of the selling entity for cash. Then some companies decided to save themselves headaches by just acquiring the assets of the selling entity. The internal revenue code threw a wrench into those plans with Internal Revenue Code (IRC) Section 368, tax-free acquisitions and transactions.

CHAPTER 9

Ways to Structure the Acquisition

There are many ways to structure a transaction, and honestly none are 'better' than the others. I know people who swear by the method of just integrating everyone into your main entity, and others who will swear by keeping the acquired company as a separate entity for at least 12 months.

From experience, the reason I do not feel there is a 'best' approach is that there are many variables which could change your approach. Maybe you are a C-corporation and they are a sole proprietorship. Maybe you a LLC and they are an S-corporation. Aside from legal structures, there are tax implications, business reasons, and strategic reasons for choosing a post-acquisition structure.

In this chapter I will discuss a few of the structures we have seen.

Here are just a handful of business transactions that appear to be identical on the surface (as far as the customers are concerned), but will have completely different tax and legal consequences down the road:

- Creation of a subsidiary to acquire only the assets of the business being acquired
- The acquisition of the common stock or equity of the business being acquired
- Leveraged transaction with a S-corporation taking out the loan for the acquisition

- Leveraged transaction with a C-corporation taking out the loan for the acquisition
- Existing business absorb the assets (customers / employees) and take on the debts of the company being acquired

This chapter will focus on the business aspect of your acquisition and structuring it from that point of view. What this chapter will <u>not</u> do is determine the best structure for tax purposes for you and your business. That is beyond the scope of this book. Frankly, despite there being many books on the subject, I would not recommend picking your specific corporate structure from a book (or article on the Internet) without speaking with your personal CPA about the implications of the structure you are selecting for your specific situation. I know millionaire's who swear by different approaches of how to do the transactions, so you need to find what is right for you and the deal.

<u>ACQUISITION FOR DEBT</u>

This method is fairly straight forward.

You and the seller determine a price. From there you can (1) give a down payment from cash on hand (or other form of 'currency,' such as stocks, land, and equity interest in another business), (2) get a loan from the bank for this purchase, or (3) have the seller finance the transaction.

If you have the cash, you have the ability to pay some or all of the purchase price.

Look at it from the seller's perspective. As we discussed earlier, there are many reasons people sell.

From a seller's point of view, they likely want to receive as much cash as they can at closing as they have other things they want to do. At the least they want to know that there is security for the cash they are getting. Sellers rarely like risk. They have a business they know and are comfortable with, and are exchanging it for something they do not know or that they perceive is out of their control. It's not always easy.

So let's say you agree on a purchase price of $1 million. How does the seller get their money?

Remember: Not all money is created equally.

GETTING INVESTORS

There are numerous books, articles and classes you can take about bringing on investors to get you the money you need for buying a business. That is not this book. This book is focused on you and your company acquiring another company without the need for bringing on investors or other partners. There are definite pros and cons to doing it this way, but again, that is outside the scope of this book.

LOAN FROM THE BANK

To be clear, the discussion of getting a loan from a bank can be used interchangeably with talking with an investment banker, getting a loan from group of private investors, getting a loan from hedge fund or Venture Capital firm, getting a loan from a credit union or private money loan, or even getting a loan from your 401k. The list of lenders goes on and on; however, the terms and loan covenants will likely be different depending on the path you go down.

I do not suggest getting a loan from friends or a family member if you can avoid it. Intermingling your personal and business lives can lead to problems. I have seen family members get into disagreements and avoid each other for years over trivial amounts of money. It is usually not about the money, it is about trust and feelings and expectations.

When it comes to getting a loan from a bank (or other professional lender) they will usually have a punch list of due diligence documents they want to see.

Some examples of items needed:

- Executive Summary - who are you, what are you doing, and why do you need the money
- Historical Financial Statements (monthly or annual P&L and Balance sheet for your company)
- Historical Financial Statements (monthly or annual P&L and Balance sheet for the company you are acquiring)
- Financial projections - for the combined company
- Organization chart
- List of competitors and any industry reports
- Tax returns for the last 3 years - for your company
- Tax returns for the last 3 years - for the company you are acquiring
- Accounts receivable and Accounts Payable aging schedule
- List of any assets and depreciation
- Audited financial statements on both your company and the company you are acquiring (if any)
- All existing debt agreements
- Any pending litigation

That is just to get started. They will usually then have additional questions.

At some point the lender will do the calculation to ensure that you can repay the loan you are applying for. So it is worth the time for you to do that calculation before you approach them. More specifically if you are asking for $10 million and the loan is 10 years, the income from the business should be able to more than pay back $1 million per year + interest + reserves + other obligations.

The best book I have found for this is Rich Russakoff and Mary Goodman's 2010 book, *Make Banks Compete to Lend You Money.* You want to create a package on how to best present your business to the bank. The book is written to help you get a loan for your existing business, but it can be applied to getting any loan. It's a short book, but the information in it is definitely worth more than they charge for it!

In the early 2000s, a business partner and I created a book (for a bank loan) similar to the one discussed above. We included examples of the work the company did, a page of customer logos so they could see with whom we worked. We had it printed in color and professionally bound at Kinko's. It looked great. I am biased, but to this day it was one of the best I have seen. He and I still talk about how that was a great package. The back of the book had good / better / best scenarios, as well as scenarios of what would happen if we were completely wrong in our estimates. We ended up getting the money we needed and the company moved forward.

Here is the table of contents for a recent money raise we did for a client:

Contents

SELLER LOAN

Let's discuss a seller note, what that means, and why would they do it. If you are already familiar with this, you might want to skip this section as we mainly present examples of what this looks like to the seller.

EXAMPLE 1

You are selling your home worth $312,500. A buyer offers you $312,500. If another buyer approaches you and says, "I would like to buy your home for $375,000; however, I would like you to seller finance the loan at a 7% interest rate. You will receive $2,500 per month as a payment on the loan." Depending on your financial (or tax) situation, you might strongly consider this. You are getting 20% more for the home. If you had sold to the original buyer for $312,500 you would have federal and state taxes on the sale and then be able to invest the proceeds.

Option 1:

Sales price	$312,500 (we presume you own it free and clear)
Let's say your taxable gain is $100,000	
Tax - capital gains	20% (will vary based on holding period, year, rest of your tax situation, etc.)
Tax - state	6% (will vary based on city, state, etc.)
Tax Due	$26,000
Your net cash to you is $312,500 - $26,000 = $286,500	

Now you have $286,500 you would like to invest. Presuming you don't want to take much risk, you could put it into an investment that yields you 4% interest.

At the end of year 1, you have:

Interest earned	$ 11,460 ($286,500 * 4%)
Principal	$ 286,500
Total Assets	$ 297,960

*This example does not factor in the taxes on the interest earned as your individual tax situation can vary.

Option 2:

Sales price $375,000 (you sell on seller financed note)
Year 1 $30,000 is what you receive ($2,500 * 12 months)
Most of this is interest $26,250 ($375,000 * 7%)

At the end of year 1, you have received $26,250 in interest and only $3,750 in principal.

You are still owed $371,250

So at the end of year 1, you have:

Interest earned	$ 26,250 ($375,000 * 7%)
Principal Received	$3,750
Promissory Note	$ 371,250
Total Assets	$ 401,250

*This example doesn't factor in the taxes on the interest earned as your individual tax situation can vary

** Since you received $3,750 of principal you would likely pay some capital gains tax on the portion of gain received

You started with the property valued $62,500 over your original offer ($375,000 offer #2 - $312,500 offer #1), and now you have assets valued almost $100,000 more ($401,250 new option # 2- $297,960 option #1).

If for some reason they stop paying on the loan, you can foreclose and take the property back and keep all the money you have received.

Why would someone do this? - You are probably wondering why someone would want to pay such an inflated value for your home. Again, there are many reasons. Maybe they believe the real estate market it poised to boom and the house will be worth $450,000 in a few years. Maybe they want to lock up your home and others on the street to approach a big developer to buy all the projects. Maybe they heard of a new project coming in close to the house and have "an in" with a company that will need a lot of rental space and they want to bump the rents up to $3,500 a month.

Very important - this illustration is just that, an illustration. There are MANY factors to consider before jumping on option 2. The first is "bird in the hand is worth two in the bush." The second is the security of the loan, value of the collateral, etc. Do you feel the property is going to appreciate (meaning if the property value is going up, then you have the ability to at least step back into a better situation than you are now if they foreclose)?

Are they able to rent it out and get rental income to ensure you are getting your payment, or can they personally cover the payment? How much do you trust them? What is your tax situation? Maybe you would rather convert your income to capital gains vs rental income.

Maybe you give them three years to secure a new home loan to pay off your loan, so you are collecting the interest in the interim and they are managing the property.

EXAMPLE 2

When I moved to Las Vegas, I was introduced to a real estate investor. I had heard he was worth hundreds of millions, some said he was worth billions.

He had purchased thousands of acres of land outside of Las Vegas for $100s of dollars per acre. He might have bought five acres for $500, but he bought them in huge parcels of land.

Despite his wealth, he was one of most humble men I have met. We would meet for breakfast once or twice a month at 6 or 6:30 am at an IHOP or a Marie Callender's. It was painfully early, and I did not live close to the ones he liked going to, but it was well worth it for all that I would learn.

He had come to control the vast majority of the land in that area. The value per acre had creeped up over the previous 10-15 years to $50,000 per acre and more. He resold the acres in five acre lots. He would say to you, "I'll sell you this five acre parcel of land for $250,000. You just need to put down $1,000, and then make principal and interest payments every month. The interest rate is 8%."

As the value of land was increasing, this was very tempting to a buyer. For only $1,000 they could acquire five acres of land and either build on it or hold it for the future. For the seller, he was now getting interest on the sales price. The interest rate of 8% was probably double what he would have gotten at a bank or through other secured investment AND the interest was being paid on the larger dollar amount (sales price). He changed the conversation from, "Can you get a bank loan and an appraisal for this amount?" to "Can you make the smaller monthly payment vs having to put down 20% on the purchase?" As a sales person, he removed the risks to they buyer (of not being able to obtain a loan).

Seller notes are obviously risky. If the collateral takes a negative turn, the seller has limited recourse other than to come back in as owner of the property.

HOW THIS APPLIES TO YOU:

The reality is, for most sellers, once they sell, the last thing they want to do is step back in and try and run the company. It is your job to make them believe that the day will never come when they will have to do that.

Tax Ramifications. Standard disclaimer: you will want to speak with your own tax adviser; this is a summary of some of the key points, it is not all inclusive. Dependent on what form the note is held in, or the size or other terms, there will be quirks in the exact treatment.

Quick Summary: This can be advantageous to a seller from a tax point of view. Depending on their tax situation, if they do a seller note, they may only pay tax when they receive the money.

From the IRS Website:

Topic 705 - Installment Sales

An installment sale is a sale of property where you will receive at least one payment after the tax year in which the sale occurs. You are required to report gain on an installment sale under the installment method unless you "elect out" on or before the due date for filing your tax return (including extensions) for the year of the sale. You may elect out by reporting all the gain as income in the year of the sale on Form 4797 (PDF), Sales of Business Property, or on Form 1040, Schedule D (PDF), Capital Gains and Losses, and Form 8949 (PDF), Sales and Other Dispositions of Capital Assets.

Situations Where the Installment Method is Not Permitted

Installment method rules do not apply to sales that result in a loss. You cannot use the installment method to report gain from the sale of inventory or stocks and securities traded on an established securities market. You must report any portion of the capital gain from the sale of depreciable assets that is ordinary income under the depreciation recapture rules in the year of the sale. For additional situations and information about when you cannot report payments on the installment method, see Publication 537, Installment Sales.

Determining Your Total Gain

Your total gain on an installment sale is generally the amount by which the selling price of the property you sold exceeds your adjusted basis in that property. The selling price includes the money and the fair market value of property you received for the sale of the property, any selling expenses paid by the buyer, and existing debt encumbering the property that the buyer pays, assumes, or takes subject to.

Reporting the Sale on Your Tax Return

Under the installment method, you include in income each year only part of the gain you receive, or are considered to have received. You do not include in income the part of the payment that is a return of your basis in the property. Use Form 6252 (PDF), Installment Sale Income, to report an installment sale in the year the sale occurs and for each year you receive an installment payment. You will need to file Form 1040 (PDF), U.S. Individual Income Tax Return, and may need to attach Form 4797 (PDF), Sales of Business Property, and Form 1040, Schedule D (PDF). You must also include in income any interest as ordinary income. For details, see **Reporting Interest**, *below.*

Reporting Interest

You generally report interest on an installment sale as ordinary income in the same manner as any other interest income. If the installment sales contract does not provide for adequate stated interest, part of the stated principal may be recharacterized as unstated interest or original issue discount for tax purposes, even if you have a loss. You must use the applicable federal rate (AFR) to figure the amount of stated principal recharacterized as unstated interest or original issue discount. The AFRs are published monthly in the Index of Applicable Federal Rates (AFR) Rulings.

Additional Information

For additional information, refer to Publication 537, Installment Sales.

Site Reference: https://www.irs.gov/taxtopics/tc705.html

How long is the seller note for?

A seller note can be for 10 days or 10 years. This is up to you to negotiate and determine. Maybe the seller wants a longer term as they think the tax rules will change for their benefit in the future. Maybe they want a longer term as they really want to leave this 'loan' to their children so they have an annuity of sorts in the future. Maybe they want a super short term, but they want it long enough that you will be paying them in the next tax year.

For example, if you are closing the transaction in November, they may say you have until January 18th to pay it off and they are hoping you do NOT pay it off before January 1st.

What interest rate will the loan be at?

The interest rate will be as low as you can get it. We once did a transaction at 0%. So even if we had the money, it would make sense to not pay it off early. More likely, though, you will have to be at least at the IRS AFR rates.

What are AFRs?

According to the IRS: *Each month, the IRS provides various prescribed* **rates** *for federal income tax purposes. These* **rates,** *known as* **Applicable Federal Rates** *(or AFRs), are regularly published as revenue rulings.*

What that means is the IRS expects you to charge interest on loans you make. If you do not charge the interest rate, they will impute it (calculate it) for you and tax you on it as if you received it.

As of this writing, AFRs are updated monthly on https://apps.irs.gov/app/picklist/list/federalRates.html. If that link does not work, search for "IRS AFR Rates." Many other websites list AFRs. Because it is such a common search item, some search engines will give you the rates without having to click through to a website. Some of these are in the 1.89% - 2.5% annual interest rate.

ANNUITY

There are many types of annuities. The basic premise is that an insurance contract that will offer a guaranteed stream of income over some period of time.

There are fixed annuities, variable annuities, deferred income annuities, and immediate annuities. Each has its own strengths and weaknesses.

For purposes of acquiring a company, an annuity can be used to settle the seller financed loan at a discount.

For example, you owe a seller $10 million. You may choose to buy an annuity for $7.5 million. That is a 25% discount off the cost of the purchase. The annuity will pay the seller $40,000 per month for 20 years (so they get $40,000 * 12 * 20 = $9,600,000) .

The seller would probably prefer having the sales income paid by a billion dollar insurance company, rather than from their (now your) company.

This lessens the risk from the transaction for the seller's family. Yes, the present value drops below $10 million, but depending on their financial situation, this steady stream of payments can give much more peace of mind and potentially much better tax ramifications.

Here's another example. You owe a seller $3 million, and they prefer a guaranteed $12,500 per month for 20 years from someone other than you. You can purchase that for $2.4 million, which you can borrow. The numbers penciled out for you at $3 million, but as you can save $600,000 (or 20%) on the loan which might be worth more of your time to focus on in the short term.

In June 2016, the Powerball lottery jackpot reached approximately $1.5 billion. The winner would have the option of either taking a one-time lump sum of $930 million, or take a slowly increasing annuity starting at $22 million per year and escalating to $92 million per year over 30 years. 96% of lottery winners take the lump sum. However when the jackpot got to this level, many 'experts' or 'financial gurus' wrote articles, and billionaires gave interviews, explaining why the winner should take the annuity. How much different will life really be with $22 million per year guaranteed vs $930 million lump sum? Is there anything you just HAVE to have that you can't get with the annuity?

Financial experts have always said you should take the lump sum, put it in nice diversified portfolios, and just live off the interest and dividends. In theory, that works great. In reality, that does not work for everyone.

Winners slowly dip into the pot and take money out here and there, and before you know it, the extrapolated spreadsheet does not make sense as people are not that disciplined. With the annuity however, no matter how much you try and screw up your spending this year, your checking account will be replenished next year with a new deposit. Believe me, that is not to say sellers will not find a way to screw that up as well, but some sellers know themselves and (aside from tax reasons) they know they will be better off with an annuity or, as they call it, an allowance of sorts to them and their family.

The selling owner of one the businesses I mentioned earlier is in his 70's and he said to me, "What would I do with all that money now anyway? If I'm getting it over time, I can put the annuity in a trust and have better controls over it so my children and grandchildren are properly taken care of. It is more of a legacy with some control that way." This seller did not want all of the money up front. He knew that if he received all the money and passed away, it was likely that his children / grandchildren would not have the discipline that he had and he was scared they would blow through it all within a couple of years. An annuity has the ability to potentially prevent that from happening.

Once you and the seller agree on a price, you need the money, and the previous section gives you some examples of where and how to find it. You will find quickly that there are different prices based on different deliverables. As I am sure you know, all cash will get you a lower price than any seller financed deal.

SIDE BAR: In 1994 the comedy *The Hudsucker Proxy* played in the theaters but was what some call a box office dud. It grossed about $3 million on a budget reported to be in the $25 - 40 million range. That being said, I found it a good movie with some very interesting business techniques you can use for acquisitions.

Partial Acquisition

You acquire a portion of the business and have the rights to acquire the remainder at some most likely point in the future, such as in 3 - 5 years.

This gives the seller two liquidity events, and allows you to know what you are buying even though you are not buying the whole thing just yet.

You would want to have majority control of major decisions so you are not running the company by committee every time something needs to get done.

POTENTIAL STRUCTURE: Some sellers would rather sell you 51% now and have the corporation 'redeem,' or buy back, their other 49%. Potentially, this can be beneficial to the seller, depending on the corporate structure of the company as well as the historical earnings. From your point of view it will not matter. You will have control at 51% ownership. Once the company redeems the other 49%, your shares will be the only shares outstanding, and you will now have 100%.

Example: imagine the seller owns 100 units. You acquire 51 units. You own 51 of 100 units, and the seller owns 49 units. Later the company buys back the seller's 49 units and retires them. There are now only 51 units remaining and you own all 51 of them.

Objection / Speed Bump: there is a saying, "you don't know what you don't know." While this sounds like a witty Yogi Berra reference, it's a simple concept: sometimes you just do not know everything. In buying a business, many times the selling owner doesn't know what they don't know. This is not a slight against them, just the reality that most business owners will likely sell their business just once in their life, so you have to be prepared that they only know what they have heard through others or, unfortunately, what they have seen in movies.

We have had many conversations with owners who say, "We grew our business to $1 million in revenue in a short period, so we are planning to grow it organically to $5 million in the same short period going forward." Again, while I wish them the best and in some industries this may work, this is few and far between.

The old adage 'the first million is the hardest,' or, as T. Boone Pickens states in his book *The First Billion is the Hardest: Reflections on a Life of*

Comebacks and America's Energy Future, once you have done something, it's easier to repeat the second time around. I will have to take T. Boone Pickens' word for it on the billionaire front, but on the millionaire front, almost all the ones I have spoken with agree.

A close friend of mine runs a very successful company in Las Vegas. He has shared a tremendous amount of wisdom with me over the years, including this advice from his mentor when he and his partner were starting out. Many entrepreneurs agree that going from $0 to $1 million is not the same as going from $1 million - $5 million and nowhere close to going from $10 million to $50 million.

Buying a portion of a company might be the way to go. In terms of structure, you would usually acquire a portion now with the right, during a defined period, to acquire the rest and/or they can sell to you at some point in the future. In this way, you become partners with the seller. "We are buying 51% for $1 million, but any time between now and 3 years from now, we can buy the other 49% for $2 million." Or, "We are buying 51% for $1 million, but any time you desire to sell the other 49%, we have the right to buy it from you for the Fair Market Value as defined by an agreed upon valuation expert." The ways this can be done are truly endless, but this usually gives the selling shareholder more comfort as they are not completely out of the day to day.

Creation of a new entity to do the deal

In his 2010 book *The 40 Hour Work Year,* Scott Fritz discusses some methods he used to grow his business to annualized revenue of over $170 million. One of the concepts he discusses in his books and presentations is the idea of PODs or Points of Distribution.

A simple explanation is: I own 100% of a company and you and I want to partner together on it. We set up a separate entity of which my company will own 60% and you will own 40%. You will function from a sales point of view to bring in the customers. However, my entity will serve as the organization that services the customer. The actual structure is set up very similar to a joint venture or a partnership; the execution of the administrative pieces are where the differences come in to play.

How this applies to you:

So let's say you speak with a company that does not want to sell, but does want to work with you. They could be a small solo practitioner or they could be a 10-person location, but they recognize the strong leverage you have with your marketing or with your connections in the industry. Maybe they are just great at sales and/or execution, but do not want to deal with the minutiae of administrative tasks.

Here is how we would set it up:

Corporate Structure

XYZ Corp is your company
Seller is Nevada John

XYZ Nevada 1, LLC setup

a. A new LLC is set up for purposes of all the assets in his company.
b. Ownership is 50% XYZ, 50% John
c. This LLC serves as a marketing arm for XYZ.
d. Customers are owned by the LLC, branded as XYZ Nevada (for example) or they just keep the same name and it's 'ABC, a XYZ Company' on the invoices.
e. All customer orders, accounting, administration, collections, etc., are handled by XYZ for a 6% management fee. **– This is optional, but I would recommend it as it will help cover your administrative costs and it is also a way to help monetize your administrative team. (I have seen this fee as high as 15% before).**
f. There is 60/40 split of profits at year end (or quarterly) between XYZ and Nevada John
g. Under this scenario XYZ should be able to streamline many of the following expenses under the XYZ umbrella which would then get

covered by XYZ under the admin fee and reduce overall expenses (to provide more bottom line profits):

i. Reduced health insurance
ii. Dues and subscriptions (we likely already pay the same ones)
iii. Telephone service discount
iv. Insurance
v. Accountant
vi. 401K professional fees
vii. Legal fees
viii. Marketing / website
ix. Trade shows
x. Should consider a buy sell agreement together based on terms you both like.

- I would suggest something similar to "Sales price to be allocated based on customers acquired listed on exhibit A/total sales, to be called "pro rata sales""
  - If sale takes place between 0 and 1 year from date of XYZ Nevada, LLC setup, then:
    o 40% of Sales price * (pro rata sales *90%)
  - If sale takes place between 1 and 3 year from date of XYZ Nevada, LLC setup
    o 40% of Sales price * (pro rata sales *75%)
  - If sale takes place between 3 and 5 year from date of XYZ Nevada, LLC setup
    o 40% of Sales price * (pro rata sales *60%)
  - If sale takes place after 5 years from date of XYZ Nevada, LLC setup
    o 40% of Sales price * (pro rata sales *50%)
  - The reason for this is people will likely buy you for (1) your systems, (2) your people, (3) your goodwill, etc. the sales value will likely only determine a portion of the sales price
  - So if in year 2 someone buys you for $10 million and the sales from customers on exhibit A are $6 million

and the total sales of XYZ are $20 million, then the Seller John will get:

- o   40% of $10 million = $4 million * 6/20 * 75% = $ 900,000, which is roughly 9% of the total sales price.

- Again, this is just an example, you DO NOT have to go with these #'s, but some variation of the above so it defines out what the value should be.

- Another approach is what one of my partners' calls a Texas Standoff - this is where XYZ would present an offer number to John for his interest and John can either take the money or he can agree to offer that exact amount to XYZ and John would then buy the entire company. This keeps both sides honest and offering the best for both.

Timeline

Here is an example of a time line you can anticipate. I have seen it go much faster (i.e. 60 days) and I've seen it drag out for 9 months.

- Month 0: Signed letter of intent
- Month 1: Drafts of agreements and defining out who is doing what post-closing; suggest having our key people meet with Seller and vice versa
- Month 2: Continued Due Diligence, reviewing Seller processes, verifying Seller #'s (at high level), meet Seller's employees, agree on integration timeline
- Month 3: Focus on finalizing the branding strategy, FAQ's for Seller's employees / your employees / Seller's customers, website prepared to switch over and any press releases
- Month 4: Closing / Launch of the two companies

Revenue Split

As far as how the numbers and revenues are split, imagine you have a seller making about 10% EBITDA after expenses and overhead. If you have the ability to move them into your space, take over their administrative pieces, reduce some dues / subscriptions, and reduce other overhead like insurances, then this might work for you:

XYZ Nevada 1 LLC

100% Revenue	$ 1,000,000
70% Costs	700,000
30% Gross Profit	300,000
6% Admin fee	(60,000)
8% Other overhead/selling expenses	(80,000)
Net Income	$ 160,000

Seller John's profit = $160,000 * 40% = $64,000

Seller John is still taking home approximately 10% of revenue.

How this plays out for you:

Admin fee	$ 60,000
Profit from LLC	96,000 (160,000 * 60%)
Profit	$ 156,000

It is important to note that your additional net profit will not be $156,000. That is the additional gross profit you will apply to XYZ's overhead. If you are able to make it so your overhead does not increase, then it would all be profit. There should be some bump up in your overhead because of the increased number of employees and customers you service. However, it should not eat away completely at your share.

Remember, the benefits of doing this are the intangibles of increased total revenue spread over your existing costs (your admin cost per revenue $ should go down), monetizing your admin department and your systems, increasing your footprint, etc.

The profit you will get from this deal will be roughly 40% less than other revenue (since Seller John is getting that), but the acquisition cost of that revenue will be next to nothing as Seller John has already invested in that, and your admin team will now be generating revenue as well.

You will want to apply this directly to your situation to see how the numbers work. Maybe your admin cost needs to be 8% instead of 6%, maybe 12%, maybe 4%, that is for you and the seller to work out. But for you, you want to understand how this will directly affect your bottom line and, more importantly, your cash flow.

Cost reductions. In the above example we used 70% for the cost. If you are in a service based business, or perhaps you have better hardware costs, then having the XYZ Nevada 1 LLC purchase directly from you can also provide XYZ with some extra cash flow. If XYZ Nevada 1 LLC pays to XYZ, LLC in 30 days and XYZ, LLC does not pay the vendor for 45 days, that extra 15 days of float time could significantly increase your cash flow.

Multiple PODs - you should start seeing a positive effect on your bottom line and your cash flow.

Imagine you are a company doing $ 3 million per year and you put 10% on the bottom line, so you have annual profit of $ 300,000.

Add on XYZ Nevada 1, LLC POD # 1 = $ 156,000 of new gross profit and let's say costs you now have $50,000 of additional overhead, so you have a net of $106,000.

Add on XYZ Nevada 2, LLC POD # 2 = this one is a little more profitable at $175,000, but has a $100,000 increase in overhead (maybe by this point you have to hire someone new to help out), so you have a net of $ 75,000.

Add on XYZ Your State, LLC POD # 3 = this one is a smaller company, but you have more savings on overhead. $175,000 gross profit, and $75,000 overhead, so you have a net of $100,000.

POD 1	106,000
POD 2	75,000
POD 3	100,000
Increased net	$ 281,000

In this example, you would have an almost 100% increase in your annual profit, the majority of which is driven by your administrative department picking up more work and putting someone else's company into your administrative machine.

<u>Tax treatment (this could change depending on structure, how owned and the tax rules at the time of the transaction).</u>

Disclaimer (again) - each person's tax situation is different, so this is just an example.

XYZ should just treat revenue as revenue. The IRS does not care if you are getting it as labor revenue or product sales or admin fees or profits from your LLC. It will all flow to XYZ's income statement.

For Seller John, depending on how the companies are set up, he might be able to take his profits and also reduce his taxable income as he is now incurring business expenses the company will no longer be covering (e.g., his travel, cell phone, health insurance, etc.).

Further, assume Seller John's LLC will now be called John 123 LLC.

He could possibly contribute the customer lists to XYZ Nevada, LLC.

So his profits could flow to his LLC and then the additional expenses could reduce his tax burden.

That is very theoretical, and Seller John's situation would determine if that makes sense for him as it depends on, among other things, his tax basis, his desires, and his long term plans.

EXAMPLE LETTER / EMAIL SENT:

Here is an example of an email laying out a pending transaction. In this scenario, one of the partners was retiring and the other was staying on. In this scenario, XYZ would be your company and TyCo would be the company you are buying:

Tyler / Collin,

Here is a brief summary of the key points of the transaction.

Once we get in agreement on this piece, then I think we will just hand it off to an attorney to draw up the operating agreement of the LLC.

Corporate Structure

- o Nevada LLC to be set up called XYZ AZ # 1, LLC, with a dba filed as XYZ
- o Ownership to be 50% TyCo / 50% XYZ

Governance

- o Decision matrix to be created, see timeline below

General points

- o _____ employees to be terminated and given severance prior to closing of transaction
- o All employees to be moved to XYZ payroll effective ____
- o Administrative tasks (handling the mail, paying the bills, renewing subscriptions, etc.) to be handled by XYZ staff.
- o Joint announcement to TyCo customers/vendors/ employees to be agreed upon
- o Monthly draw of $8,000 to be paid to TyCo and to XYZ every month by the 15th of the month following the month closed
- • i.e. June draw to be paid by July 15th

- Quarterly 'true up' of budget to be done to insure in line with annual budget of $250,000 of net income.
- Draw can be increased upon agreement by both parties or if the LLC is ahead of budgeted net income by more than 20%
- By January 1, should have at least 30 days working capital built up in the company
o After calendar year 2016, XYZ to provide to TyCo a reconciliation of what actual labor service cost incurred towards the LLC was and if less than 68%, then the 70% amount will be adjusted down to the actual amount. If costs are greater than 70%, then the amount will be adjusted up.
- If for some reason TyCo and XYZ do not agree on the calculation, the POD will hire an independent 3rd party to determine the 70% service rate being used if it needs to be adjusted

Expenses paid by the POD

o Consulting contract for Collin through TyCo for:
- $ 10,500 per month consulting
- $ 1,000 per month for car, parking, repairs, gas, etc.
- $ 700 per month for meals and entertainment with customers
- $ 500 per month for mileage and cell phone
- Expectations are Collin to bring in $250,000 per year in new customers (i.e. $50K annual contracts x 5 customers)
o The POD will be allocated any / the cost for any products sales.
o All direct expenses for the POD
- Office expenses, taxes, legal, bank fees, permits, marketing, insurance (not health), client specific expenses, etc.
o Any travel expenses incurred directly related to the LLCs customers and/or XYZ and Collin joint travel for executive meetings.

- o Cost of Annual tax return
- o XYZ to receive 70% of service revenue
- • Amount to be paid based on invoiced amounts.
- • Should the service revenue become bad debt expense, then the POD will reimburse XYZ on the losses

Breakout Examples # 1, no bad debt:

- o LLC invoices customer $10,000
- o XYZ invoices POD $6,000
- o LLC paid $10,000, XYZ invoice paid

Breakout Examples # 2, partial bad debt:

- o LLC invoices customer $10,000
- o XYZ invoices POD $6,000
- • LLC only paid $8,000, XYZ invoice paid for $6,000

Breakout Examples # 3, full bad debt:

- o LLC invoices customer $10,000
- • XYZ invoices POD $6,000
- • LLC paid $0, LLC will have a loss of $6,000 and the XYZ invoice will be paid from future profits since XYZ has fronted the labor costs

Expenses paid by XYZ

- o Service labor
- o Payroll taxes
- o Health insurance
- o Customer required contract labor
- o Any direct labor attributable to servicing the customer
- o Bookkeeping and accounting for the POD (not including outside tax prep fees)
- o Software licenses (phone and Internet for the office)

Calendar / Timeline

<u>Week of June 6th</u>

- o Finalize summary and timeline
- o Decision matrix drafted with the POD of who is doing what. Lion share will be on XYZ's shoulders, just need clarity on what items Collin wants to be a part of
- o Hire attorney to draft LLC and operating agreement – estimated cost <$ 2,500
- o Inclusive of setting up the LLC and state filing fees
- o TyCo to discuss with their personal CPA on structure of contribution of customer list for 50% interest in the LLC

<u>Week of June 13th</u>

- o FAQ's for employees / vendors / customers drafted (we have most of this done already)
- o Discussion with marketing team about how to handle announcement
- o Ordering of business cards for the 'new' employees of XYZ
- o Draft press releases and/or letters to vendors etc.

<u>Week of June 20th</u>

- o Final review of documents
- o Paperwork with payroll company for new employee hires, if needed
- o Set up of bank account
- o Collin to plan trip to New Orleans for week of July 5th to meet everyone with his 'integration team'

The reason the POD works out in this case is it helps get over a mental hurdle for the seller. The valuation piece is not a numerical piece as much a feeling of giving up something for nothing. This is where the seller needs to understand you are helping them diversify, that being part of bigger company should yield higher multiple for everyone, that the money they are paying you for admin fees is actually increasing their profits, and that they are being given opportunity to grow and sell.

Consider presenting something to them along the lines of, "What I'm proposing is something where we manage the entire business for 7% management fee and you keep 85% of the profits until you gets $xxxx." (Pick a number close to what they believes the value is.) You will want to run the #'s, but this should get you the lion share of the revenue and more profits. You can even state that once they receive a certain amount, the profit split moves back to 50/50. I have seen some service-based companies where the admin fee + the small percent of profits was all they needed to make it work. Each industry will be different, so just check your numbers.

Either of the above deals usually work for both parties. However, the latter (with the 85% of profits) will 'feel' like a better deal for them. For you, though, remember -- you are getting 6% - 8% of the top line revenue, which on a business earning 15%, is like getting 50% of the bottom (net income) (ex. $100K * 15% = $15,000 * 50% = $7,500, which is approximately your $6,000 -$8,000 admin fee.

Pros to discuss

- By setting it up this way, you are also likely giving them the ability to offer more services / products to their existing customers, which means more money for them.
- Also stress 'this is being done to help alleviate much of the stress and risk you carry as a 100% owner, so you can spend more time with your family or doing other things such as developing more PODS'
- By giving them the ability to make $ off of other PODS, they can make more $ not only in the short term, but from aggregate wealth vs if you just cut them a check for his business.
- While for some it is not a huge deal, remember, from a tax point of view this could benefit them more in the long term then if someone just cutting a check at closing.

An important thing we have found is that sellers may "feel" that they are not getting anything, but you are. That is where you need to go through all you are doing, including an estimate of the amount you expect to spend to make it a success, the potential marketing money you are going to spend to help out, etc. Sell the vision of the company. It should not be about the next 30 days, sell them what you are doing over the next year, three years, five years. If your goal is to build it up and sell to a large private equity firm or public company within three years, tell them that. Be honest with them. You want them 100% bought in to your vision so you are all moving in the same direction. Show them your vision statement, your core values, your long term plan, etc.

You will need to make them see that they are getting the first bite at the apple and the lion share of the new revenue. Show them (with numbers) how you only make money if you perform.

The benefit to your company is increased volume, revenue, monetizing your systems more, and increasing of the overall value of your company and the multiple you can command. The additional money from profits is an extra. You are not setting this up to take the revenues they are already bringing, but to increase the pie and share in that increase.

Remember, it just takes a small increase to significantly increase the size of the pie.

From math class, remember the formula for the area of a circle. If you are looking at the amount of pie or pizza that you get, look at these two examples.

- The area of an 8 inch pizza is 50.26 square inches
- The area of a 10 inch pizza is 78.5 square inches. (56% larger than an 8 inch)

What additional overhead you should plan for

Look through your financial statements and what expenses do you have on a per user basis.

Internet - probably not

Software Licenses - maybe

Rent - no

Utilities - no

Payroll processing fees - possible slight increase

Advertising - yes

Insurances - possibly yes

Bank fees - no

Contractor fees - no

Training - yes

Legal - possibly yes

Compensatory:

- Need to determine if the seller is getting on your payroll, if they only get paid as a normal commissioned sales person would, or just through profits. This will likely be driven by how they currently handle it and what role they anticipate serving going forward
- Salary – do they get one now? They will likely want/need to keep getting one.
- Bonuses – do they get any based on hitting certain revenue/EBITDA targets? This is commonly not in place as they are partners in the deal, so their bonus will be as increased profits (and you likely are not getting bonuses either). There is the potential of an additional bonus for negotiating and completing more PODs. However, their primary focus should be on sales. One time a sales person was so focused on finding additional PODs, he was neglecting to perform other operational tasks inside the company so that department started to suffer.

Governance:

Your company (XYZ) should be the managing partner or managing member of the LLC and have final decision making authority on all customer selection, business processes, etc. If the company is going to be branded with your company name, you will likely want to run it like you run your other business to keep things as efficient as possible.

Claw back / bonus option:

From experience, one addition I have found helpful to introduce early on is a stipulation that if the sales drop below $xxxx within the first 12 months, then there is an adjustment to the profit split / admin fee / etc. (i.e. more your way). This figure should be something like 80% of the prior year's figure. A number that you would be happy with, but something they will agree should be easy to hit. If they do not believe they will hit 80% of the revenue they are representing, that sends a message to you that they are not as confident as they should be.

Feel free to put in something for their benefit as well. Something that says that if he or she is able through sales efforts to bring an additional $yyyy per year in revenue, they get an extra bonus. This number can be 20% or something measurable. We have omitted this when they were coming on to payroll and we already had the compensatory piece in place.

Expectations:

Some expectations about "life after signing" should be discussed. I would just call them up (or go to lunch) and walk through the list and ask what their expectations are:

- How frequently do the both of you meet in person? I recommend at least quarterly for the first year.
- Monthly financial statements provided to both of you.
- What expenses does the LLC have to eat vs them personally – this will be a big thing as most sole owners run everything through the business. We had one acquisition where the former owner was storing their Christmas and Halloween decorations, as well as a storage trailer, in the warehouse, so we needed to get that removed. That minor detail turned out to create an issue between him and our CFO as the seller viewed it as it was still his company and he didn't like being told what to do.

- What subscriptions (magazine, dues, technology licenses, research tools) do they have and/or think is necessary which you think aren't?
- What conferences / groups / organizations should the organization pay for vs should be paid personally? We had some CPA firms that required the entity to pay for the partners' state licenses and others which expected partners to pay them out of their own pocket.
- Communication criteria and/or cultural expectation; how frequently?
- The messaging delivered to customers – this needs to be defined out, as discussed in other chapters.
- FAQ's for employees / vendors / customers – as discussed in other chapters.
- Pro-rata treatment of any existing licenses or subscriptions and/or how to treat those that you both have paid for. Some of these licenses when you cancel them may give a refund. Who gets the refund?

I realize some of these may seem like trivial items or expenses, but I have seen blow up arguments over a $450 per year license that the seller and new owners did not agree was needed. This was to pay for a service the new owners did not see as a good return on investment, whereas the seller had ALWAYS paid it through the business so felt it was required.

Focus

Your focus should continue to be on what you are providing to the seller in exchange for them doing the deal with you.

"In exchange for our admin fee and percentage of profits, you are (1) able to focus at work as a visionary, (2) potentially double your revenue from customers with the additional services we offer such as _____ and _____, (3) remove you from the majority of administrative and accounting functions, (4) allow you to participate in revenue of other PODS you introduce us to and we pick up, and (5) shift your day to day responsibilities and most important, risk from you to XYZ".

Once you can get that message across, it should be easier for them to see how this is a great deal for both parties.

Cash on sale - what happens if you sell the whole company, what happens to the POD?

So you have the POD in place and you have stated your vision is to sell to someone else within three years.

Now that time comes. The buyer says, "Hi we love what you are doing at XYZ Company, we would like to buy XYZ for $10 million."

The buyer does not care how you split that $10 million between the different PODs you have, they just want it all.

As discussed elsewhere, this is where you need to define this in advance. A buy-sell agreement on your individual POD LLC will usually have these areas covered.

What we did in some cases was say to the seller, "We are going to be a 60/40 POD, with us owning 60%. Your 40% is worth $400,000 today. If the company is sold in the future, you will get that $400,000." Some sellers were fine with that.

For the majority of the deals we did, this was not as much of an issue as re-selling was far off in the future.

- In one deal we agreed upon a pre-defined percent of any subsequent sales price that seller would get. Word of caution here: this provides the least protection for you in case they do nothing after you buy them. This is basically making them a partner in the deal. First instinct may make sense, but this comes with a lot of pitfalls.

  o You can try and shield this by saying, "If you are working with the company at the time of sale, then you get 15% of the net sales price." That 15% is based on a rough estimate of the value of their company compared to your value at the time of the transaction.

- o Again, this opens you up to many challenges if they decide to retire and you spend another five years growing the business. In this case, you would also want to define what 'net sales price' means, such as after legal fees, payments of debts, etc. Otherwise they could end up making more than you in the sale!
- o A strong attorney should be engaged to help draft the buy sell agreement for you.

- For one acquisition, we offered a small percentage of revenue (3 – 5%) every year for five years as their payout. If we sold during that time, we would calculate what that amount was and it would be paid off at closing.
- Another option is that upon the sale of the entire XYZ Company, you will have a purchase price analysis done (which will probably cost $7,500 - $10,000). You split the fee and they will get their portion based off of what the analysis says their portion of the customer list is worth. While this is a better approached, there are potential issues here in that they may argue they do not like the methodology or calculation used, etc. You need to define how the valuation expert is picked. A common approach is for each party to pick an expert and then the values are averaged. Or, you can have a third party make the choice.

Keep it as simple so both parties can agree to the valuation. For the CPA firms, we looked at a normal CPA firm could sell for 1.1 x revenue. So we said with our PODS, that on a sale, the value of the POD would be 0.9 x revenue for that POD and they would get their respective percentage. The reason for the disparity between the 1.1x and the 0.9 x is the intangible value we were bringing to the table and to allow the arbitrage for our entity for doing the deal.

In general, I recommend establishing a ceiling on what that value can be now, even if they will be active in the business. If this is the case, they will likely not like this "call" feature, which allows you to buy them out in the future for a price that is pre-defined now. In one case we found it helpful to separate out for valuation calculations what the value is of customers that exist as of the date of closing, and those that come to the POD after closing. The latter are not 100% through the efforts of the seller, so those should not be worth as much.

The value should obviously be non-recourse, meaning if that specific POD fails for whatever reason or gets sued and goes under, then you / XYZ are not liable to pay them for that value.

To be clear, you are setting up a NEW business. It will have the same name (kind of), same business services, same operations, but it is a new business with new owners (you and them), so you want to get most of this done on the front end.

EXAMPLE:

POD # 1 owned 60% by CPA Firm and 40% by seller.

Seller had a $ 400,000 tax practice, operates heavily in the business. As a sole practitioner, we would likely offer them a 10 - 15% referral fee for 5 - 7 years, or set up like a POD. They are not ready to sell, so we set up a POD.

Year 1:

CPA Firm has $ 4,000,000 in revenue
POD #1 has $ 400,000 in revenue

Year 5:

CPA Firm has $ 5,000,000 in revenue
POD # 1 has $ 500,000 in revenue

Offer to buy the company at 1.1 x revenue, so $5,500,000

CPA Firm needs to buy out the 40% of POD # 1 from the Seller.

Value of the 40% is:

$ 400,000 of revenue brought to the company * 0.9 = $360,000 * 40% = $ 144,000

$ 100,000 of additional revenue brought to the company * 0.75 = $ 75,000 * 40% = $ 30,000

Total value = $ 174,000

Had they sold to us on a referral fee and retired, we might have expected attrition of 10% per year (i.e. the revenue declines 10% per year), so the amount they would have made would have been:

Year 1	$ 400,000 * 15% =	60,000
Year 2	360,000 * 15% =	54,000
Year 3	324,000 * 15% =	48,600
Year 4	292,000 * 15% =	43,740
Year 5	262,000 * 15% =	39,366
Total		$ 245,706

The seller may say, "I could be making $245,700 if you just buy me out now." Well yes, but that $245,706 is paid over the next 5 years, with the POD concept we are offering, you will get your current salary + less work and admin (as we are handling it) + 50% of the profits each year + the $174,000 sales price if we grow based on the above.

In this scenario, the seller would be much better off going with the POD route, and for a seller not planning on retiring, this is a great solution.

<u>Royalty Deal</u>

This is the simplest method, but not the most likely structure.

If this makes you think of Kevin O'Leary on *Shark Tank*, then you are right.

I spoke with a 70-year-old absentee owner whose business had revenues of over $15 million. In looking at his financial statements, I determined he was generating a net income of about 5% of the bottom line of his financial statements.

After discussing his goals with him - retirement - and determining that the compensatory piece was not critical for him, I suggested a royalty structure.

Side bar: in terms of products, services, and solutions, our company had twice the offering he had at his company; he product offering was in one vertical. For us, this was a great way to get more qualified sales people.

We discussed that his value multiple would normally be 5x of EBITDA. I told him that we would offer him 5% of the revenue for 7 years. This would, in essence, give him the same personal income as his business is generating (5% of revenue) for the next 7 years. This would be a customer list sale.

This was positive for him because by offering more products / services to the customers, he would participate in the additional revenue.

For us, we were essentially taking over his sales team and just paying a 'referral fee' for the customers.

You might be wondering why he would do such a deal. But realize that his motivation was not selfish. He had been in the business for over 40 years and wanted to create something that would take care of the employees. He was still going to make the same money, but he did not have to take the risk or deal with the headache of running the company.

In a transaction with a CPA firm, we also structured it this way. However, we capped the amount to be paid. The amount was capped at well over a value on a straight sale. In a normal sale, he would have sold his business for $400,000. We said we would pay him up to $480,000 for his business based on this structure. He was confident enough in his client base that they were not going to go anywhere. Thus he was able to earn an additional 20%.

You might be saying to yourself, "That sounds crazy, I would never sell my company for something like that," but the reality is, I have seen structured payments / installment sales more frequently than straight cash offers. There is much less risk for the buyer, so they are willing to pay more for this.

Example:

Presume you own a 3-bedroom rental property across from a college in your town. Let's say you have it completely paid off, and you could get $500,000 for it. You have owned it for 20 years and have never had it vacant more than 1 month as the school is an endless supply of tenants. Now imagine that because of your age (or situation), you need to sell the home. Not because of money, but because based on your financial plan you want to eliminate or cut down on the number of rental properties. You don't need the money to survive. Now imagine someone says to you, " I will give you $600,000 for the home, guaranteed by me and my business and the rental property. For payment, you will get 20% of the rents that are collected until it is paid off. I will manage the property 100%, and you will get checks by the 8th of each month." For some of you, you would just take the $500,000 and do something else. First off, that may not even be an option, but again, put yourself in the shoes of the seller. If they run their numbers and determine the IRR (internal rate of return) on this transaction will get them 10% on their money, as well as better tax treatment on the sale and easier estate tax planning, then why wouldn't they?

Don't ask yourself, "Why would I do this?" Ask yourself, "Why would they do this?' In many cases you will come up with a good reason why.

CHAPTER 10

Expectations to Discuss

Some of the topics you should discuss with the Seller are:

How are they expected to help in transition?

If they are going to be employed by you, what will be their role? What will be their title? What are your specific expectations of them? In the 2008 book *Who* by Geoff Smart and Randy Street, the subject of creating a scorecard for existing and potential employees is addressed. This is the perfect time to address this with the seller. They can participate in the process, but you want to be assured you are getting out of it what you want.

It might look like this:

- Seller expected to introduce all customers over $10,000 per year in sales to newly assigned internal customer contact within 30 days.
- Seller expected to attend service calls at least twice during the first 6 months to all customers over $100,000 per year in sales
- New customer sales of Monthly Recurring Revenue customers of at least $5,000 per month.
- Participate in at least 12 industry luncheons during the calendar year.
- Introduce company to three competitors for potential for acquisition before September 30th.

- Work with marketing to publish at least six articles in industry publications or online blogs before July 31ˢᵗ.

This is just an example, but figure out what strategies work for your company and include them here.

Salary

You will want to treat this like you would any other new hire. They should not be paid more than they pulled out prior to the sale. If anything, they could be paid less, as you are making payments to them on the business. I would not make this a deal breaker unless the seller is being unreasonable in their request for a specific salary. The number will likely be driven by what they are doing for the company and the value they represent.

If the seller's role is strictly to ease the transition for customers, I would not expect them to draw a significant salary. Part of the purchase price implies there is a transition period where they will help retain the customers. It is in their best interest as well as your best interest.

Decision Matrix

If the seller is not getting all of the cash upfront or is carrying a seller note, they usually want to have some control (or at least feel like they have the control), but you should define early on what that looks like.

Here is an example you can use with the company you are buying. For bigger companies it might be more restrictive, and for small ones it might require them to take on more of the load.

Figure out what they are good at and make that be the only thing they are able to make decisions on:

	Your Company	Selling Shareholder
Accounting	X	

Item		
Approval of any purchase with greater than $10,000 annual cost		X
Approval of customer order with margin less than 40%	X	
Approval of expenses under $10,000 annual cost	X	
Approve new hire	X	
Change in benefits	X	
Company Branding	X	
Company Financial Reporting	X	
Compensation plan	X	
Financial Planning	X	
Human Resources	X	
Inventory Management	X	
IT	X	
IT Direction, Equipment and Logistics	X	
Legal	X	
Marketing		X
Operations		X
Pay changes	X	
Review expense reports	X	
Sales	X	
Site location Analysis	X	
Taxes	X	
Terminate employees	X	
Website		X

The seller might want a say in your operation, or they might want approval over certain transactions. It is best to define this early on in the process. We completed a transaction, and even though there was agreement as to what their role would be post-transaction, one of the sellers still felt it was "their" company and they continued to pester me, as well as the CFO and COO with financial and operational questions outside their realm of interest.

I do not believe they were trying to hinder the process. I actually believe they thought they were helping. But they were extremely disruptive, and it got to the point that no one wanted to deal with them.

Defining up front what areas they can be involved with will save you many headaches down the road. For most acquisitions, the selling shareholders are great to work with, focused on their area and things go great for both the existing employees and the merged-in employees. I expect that allocating enough time during discussion to evaluate where people are from, how you are introduced, personality studies, and other employee issues, that you can avoid many problems. However, it is best to plan for the worst, so that if something should come up, you are able to handle it easily and sanely.

Meetings available for attendance

The seller might have attended ANY meeting at the company during the last 20 years, and if you do not discuss this early on, it will be highly uncomfortable to have that conversation after they have walked into a meeting in which they do not belong.

It can be as simple as, "Mario, with the acquisition, we want you focused on sales and business development. I do not want you spending all of your time in all the meetings. The meetings I would like you to attend are the (1) Daily Huddle, (2) all staff meetings, and (3) sales budgeting meetings."

Unless you are planning on making them an owner with those privileges, if they push back and say they want to go to the company budgeting or partner meetings, remind them, "This is why you are selling to us, so you do not have to focus on those type of items." It might be a good idea if, early on, you take them to lunch once a month and update them on all the areas you feel comfortable sharing with them. But this is something that should be addressed when you are doing the decision matrix. You likely are hoping to get a selling owner who will just leave you alone, but that is not usually the case, and the selling owner will have some good ideas every now and then that are worthy of the 45 minutes lunch.

What can they reveal publicly?

If you are a public company, there are pre-defined topics that can and cannot be discussed.

I would imagine most of the readers of this book are private companies, and for those, it is up to you what can be discussed publicly. However, those points should be agreed upon. Consider having a set couple of sentences explaining what each person can reply to specific questions.

There are some Frequently Asked Questions (FAQ) examples at the end of the book that can be used, but if you do not want to have wind taken out of the sails of your announcement, you and the seller need to be saying the same thing about why the transaction was done.

A key point to remember when bringing on a seller as an employee is that they are now representing your brand. If they had a bad reputation, you likely would not be bringing them on as an employee. Just as the seller will make sure and raise the financial considerations before the deal is done, it is your job to make sure to raise all of the operational considerations that could occur after. You likely have two different views of what that will look like, but it is your company and your brand, so discuss it with them.

Lastly, you want to discuss what you should do if you feel they are not living up to their part of the deal or they are slacking on the job. Yes, you already know what YOU want to do and will do, but you should ask them the question, so that if you ever get to that point, you can remind them that you asked early on and you have to stick with what was agreed. This obviously goes both ways and you want to give them ability to voice displeasure with you if they feel it. That is much better than them talking people outside the company or worse poisoning your employees by talking with them about it.

CHAPTER 11

Valuation

I was invited to speak to a Business class at the University of Nevada - Las Vegas on the topic of valuation. We started by going around the room to find out, "What result are you most looking forward to by the end of this session?"

The list below summarizes about 95% of the information they wanted to know:

1. How do you value a business before investing in it?
2. How do you value a company before trying to buy it?
3. How do you value intangible items, such as goodwill?
4. How do you value pre-revenue companies?
5. What are absolute deal killers that you have seen in businesses?

In this chapter we will discuss these questions.

Valuation

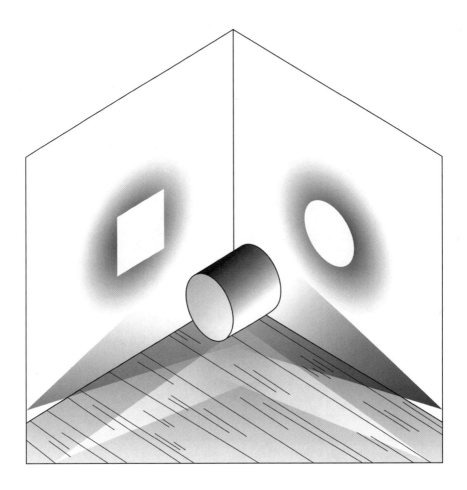

How something appears is a matter of perspective…

A picture can perfectly tell a story. Imagine a cylinder in the corner of a room. The cylinder has two lights shining on it. The first is on the short end of the cylinder, creating a shadow of a circle on the wall behind. The second light is on the long end of the cylinder, creating a square shadow on the adjacent wall. "How something appears is a matter of perspective…"

That is so true. What is of value to me will 99 times out of 100 might be of value to you, or at least not to the same degree.

A nice bottle of wine is of value to me. An expensive cigar or cup of coffee is of zero value to me. (Actually, I take that back, even though I have never had a cup of coffee in my life, the smell of Community Coffee Breakfast Blend when I make a cup for my wife in the morning is amazing.)

That will be the case with business owners you are in negotiations with as well.

My first job was wrapping gifts in my mother's Hallmark store. Later I worked at my father's law firm. Each day he would have me set aside an hour to listen to book on tapes. Many of these were motivational tapes, sales techniques, power of persuasion, how to do your best, etc. After many weeks of Zig Ziglar, Earl Nightingale, and Dr. Norman Vincent Peale tapes, he also had me listen to *Think and Grow Rich* by Napoleon Hill. As I got older, I continued this desire for learning. I discovered the 1910 book by Wallace D. Wattles, *The Science of Getting Rich*. The author of the book (and movie) *The Secret* said that this was her inspiration. *The Science of Getting Rich* came out two years before *The Master Key System*, by Charles Haanel (1912) and 27 years before *Think and Grow Rich*. These three books are must reads for anyone in business and all hit on the topic of valuation (among other items).

Other than *The Bible*, I have probably read and suggested *The Science of Getting Rich* to more people than any other book. You might even find a .pdf version of it on the Internet for free. If you do not want to read, you can download an audio version for less than $2. In deciding upon one or two quotes from the book to share, this section on 'value' was most telling:

Quote 1: *The paper, ink, and other material in this book may not be worth the money you pay for it; but if the ideas suggested by it bring you thousands of dollars, you have not been wronged by those who sold it to you; they have given you a great use value for a small cash value.*

Quote 2: *Let us suppose that I own a picture by one of the great artists, which, in any civilized community, is worth thousands of dollars. I take it to Baffin Bay, and by "salesmanship" induce an Eskimo to give a bundle of furs worth $ 500 for it. I have really wronged him, for he has no use for the picture; it* *has no use value to him; it will not add to his life. But suppose I give him a gun worth $50 for his furs; then he has made a good bargain. He has use for the gun; it will get him many more furs and much food; it will add to his life in every way; it will make him rich.*

- Wallace D. Wattles, 1910
The Science of Getting Rich

I would like to take a step back from valuing a business to something easier to grasp. I want to discuss the lifetime value of a customer (if you do not already, eventually you will view a business in your industry as your customer). Not all customers, just one customer. Let us determine how much 'value' that customer brings in in terms of pure dollars and cents.

Example 1

The average revenue you get from a customer is $5,000 per transaction.

The profit on that revenue is approximately 30%, or $1,500.

The customer needs your service every quarter, so you see them 4 times per year.

Your 'profit' per year is $1,500 * 4 = $6,000

You know from experience the average life of a customer with your company is 3.5 years.

So you know the average customer is worth $6,000 * 3.5 = $21,000.

** NOTE ** this is just from a straight perspective of <u>direct</u> value to your financial statements.

In an <u>indirect</u> value point of view, you can see how there are many other factors.

Does your relationship with that customer provide you other benefits?

- if it is a restaurant, do you get discounts you can pass on to your employees?
- is it a large, well-known customer in your city so that just including them on your list of customers gives you increased credibility?

Is that customer indirectly related to a much larger customer?

- if you are a service business, did your small contract with one customer help you land a much larger customer? For example, in a CPA firm you do the tax return of a VP at a company for $2,000 and also have their other entities as customers for an additional $20,000 in work.
- if you are an IT service provider, does the customer who pays $500 per month also serve on the board of a local charity with 10 other businesses with whom you have been trying to get your foot in the door ?

As you can see, each 'customer' can provide much more value than just their own transaction.

If you are a restaurant, the one customer you have has huge effects. According to the American Express Global Customer Service Barometer in 2010, consumers will tell on average nine (9) people about a good meal at your restaurant while they will tell approximately sixteen (16) about a bad meal.

VALUE OF A COMPANY

The business has a value now, and a value once you sprinkle the pixie dust of your company processes, marketing techniques, and additional services on it.

There are only three ways to grow your revenue.

(1) Get more customers
(2) Get customers to buy more frequently
(3) Get customers to spend more when they buy

As a general rule, if you are able to increase any (or all) of the above, your sales will grow. When evaluating a potential business, given the above, are there ways you can increase transactions from 4 times per year to 5 times per year? Can you increase the fees (or reduce your costs) to get more profit out of a transaction?

As an example, if you are able to get the average customer to purchase 4.4 times per year? Yes, I know they can't buy .4 times in a year, that's why I said on average, that is a 10% increase. We will presume for this example that you are unable to change your revenue or your costs (remember they will be hyper-sensitive to potential cost increases with your new ownership). Let us also presume you are able to keep the average customer for 4 years instead of 3.5 years because you will bump up the service level to the customer. (See chapter on Integration).

Now let's see what that will do to the value of each customer.

Example 1 - revised under your direction

The average revenue you get from a customer is $5,000 per transaction (presuming no adjustment to revenue).

The profit on that revenue is approximately $1,500 (presuming no adjustment to cost).

The customer needs your service every quarter, so you see them 4.4 times per year. (10% more often on average).

Your 'profit' per year is $1,500 * 4.4 = $6,600.

You know from experience that the average life of a customer with your company is 4.0 years (which is 0.5 years longer than from the previous company).

So you know the average customer is worth $6,600 * 4.0 = $26,400.

New customer value $ 26,400

| Original customer value | 21,000 |
| Increase in value | $ 5,400 |

25.7% increase in value

Now extrapolate this out to all of the customers they have.

Other factors in determining value

What other service can you offer to their customers?

How can their employees improve what you have?

- If they have 10 amazing employees and you would pay $20,000 to a head hunter for one of them, the value of those employees is at least $200,000 to you.

What type of volume discounts or better payment terms with vendors?

- If you represent 5% of your vendors' sales, then buy your competitor and now combined you make up 10% of your vendors' sales, negotiating payment terms to get an extra 10 days could increase your overall company cash flow dramatically.

Maybe they have four people in their accounting department and so do you. Do you really need eight people in your combined entity? Even a one or two person reduction in people will save you close to $100,000 in payroll, taxes, and benefits.

Is their average employee 'better' than yours? Better can be defined as more experience, more education, larger network, or more efficient.

Again, what is valuable to you may not represent value to them.

In January 2012, Shark Tank aired an episode in which Steve Gadlin, a web developer from Chicago, was pitching his idea for "I Want to Draw a Cat for You." The premise is, you go on his website, pay him $10 and he will draw a cat and mail it to you. Seemed completely random, but Mark Cuban ended up investing $25,000 for 33%. When the other sharks asked him 'why' with confused faces, Cuban responded, "It's hard to find talented people."

You might not be buying someone for their revenue or for their customers, you may just want their employees or some other intangible asset which is valuable to you and your business.

So what do THEY value?

This is what you have to find out.

- Do they value traveling and free time?
- Do they value security in the future?
- What about the legacy they are leaving for their children?
- Maybe all they want to do is sell!

Summary and recurring theme: Not all money is created equal!

What else can you offer which they may not get from another buyer?

- Removal of personal guarantee
- Pension plan
- Keep employees on
- Key person life insurance policy
- Get them off of their building loan
- Peace of mind
- Business to expand into your city with the right partner
- Maybe the minority partner wants to get rid of the majority partner and doing deal will help facilitate that

For many of our acquisitions, time was a major factor. We had it, they did not. We could look at a longer runway of a five- or seven-year payout, where they were ready to retire and wanted to see something in less than three years.

As an example, here are some items of value to investors which are NOT equal:

- Value to private investor with sales price amount being 5%-10% of assets
  - Many investors will consider this a larger portion of their investment so they do not want to take much risk.

- Value to private investor with sales price amount being 0.01% of assets
  - In this case, their appetite for more risk may be there. So the value will be worth more if there is a larger potential upside.

- Value to private equity lender
  - Their private equity firm may have a value attributable more towards security of funds and lower rate of return.

- Value to public company, P/E Ratio
  - The industry multiple may be higher.

If you can find an arbitrage between the above, that is where you can make money

As an example, if you can find a business that has an industry multiple in the private sector of 3 - 5 x EBITDA, but in the public company sector is 7 - 10x EBITDA, then this is your arbitrage opportunity.

What outside factors are chiming in?

What other potential buyers are they talking with?

Do they own the building they are in? If so, how is the real estate market in their area?

A CPA who owned his own stand-alone building was going to give us his practice if we would just buy the building as it was under water for him and it was causing stress for him and his wife.

Another business owner wanted to sell us his business at a low valuation, but wanted us to sign a longer term lease on the building he owned.

Figure out what other noise they are hearing and what other variables they are dealing with on a daily basis.

Deal Killers

These are items that may come up that are usually insurmountable in getting over them to make the deal work. Sometimes they are personality issues, but many times they are financial in nature.

Deal killers usually revolve around financial statements. If you sign an NDA and then request financial statements, it should not take more than a couple days to get something to review. If the target company says, "We haven't been reviewed by our internal accounting team," or "They are in draft form," then no problem. That's fine. If the financial statements are messy, but you can validate the revenue / expenses and cash flow and recreate estimates, that actually could be a benefit as you should be able to see immediate value.

If weeks become a month and still nothing, or you receive financial statements that have errors…..to me, that is a red flag.

Much of this can be handled during due diligence, but you may need to hire an outside accountant to give you a clean set of financial statements to see what you are getting involved with. Remember, poorly kept financial statements are not a deal breaker, but if the company owners are hiding something, or you do not have a good gut feeling, then that is a completely different story.

It is also helpful to have a notepad with you and jot down specific things they have said and represent. If they indicate a big project for a customer, you may want to validate it is an existing customer and not just a potential one. If they have extended or amended payment terms with a debtor, you certainly want to validate that the amendment is in writing.

Valuation metrics and multiples

Each industry has their own metric. Some are based on a multiple of revenue. Some are based on a multiple of EBITDA. Some pre-revenue models are based on number of customers or subscribers. Some are based on Monthly Recurring Revenue.

You should find what to look for fairly easily if you search the Internet. Or, if you find a public company in the industry you are evaluating, their annual reports and/or analyst reviews of their business will likely include these details. It is helpful if you become acclimated with where this financial information on the industry (or the company) can be found and do your own digging or hire an outside consultant to summarize it for you.

Industry publications will have articles with the information you're looking for, especially during the last few years. Another simple approach is to just call a business broker and say, "I am looking to purchase a car wash business, do you have any for sale? How are they valuing their business, based on what type of multiple?"

Just because a multiple is 'standard' in an industry does not mean you have to stick to it. You want to know this as this is the mindset you will most likely be walking into. So you want to understand what language you will need to be negotiating from, and what your starting point will be.

It is **a lot** easier for you to speak in the terms they are familiar with, than for you to try and convince them in terms you are used to using. If they value their business based on a multiple of revenue, you will have a hard time getting them to see why you are valuing them based on multiple of EBITDA. They will always go back to compare your method to the number is under theirs. If they feel that based on their monthly recurring revenue they are worth $XXX, then just because you have done an analysis based off of sales at $YYY, which will likely not be of as much interest.... unless, of course, it gives them a higher valuation.

Control your ego

In the early 1950's, Walt Disney acquired about 300 acres of land to build Disneyland in California. A decade later, Disney wanted somewhere else America to build on more land. The search was called Project X, and the plan was to use secret corporations and attorneys from around the country to buy up relatively worthless pieces of land. The first acre of land cost them about $80.00. They continued to buy land until June, 1965, when the *Orlando Sentinel* reported that over 27,000 acres of land had recently changed hands. Rumors started about what company was buying up all the land. In October, 1965, a reporter found out it was Walt Disney and revealed to the public, and the price of land went up over 1,000% overnight. Walt Disney still wanted to buy more, and told his brother, "Wouldn't you want to own more acres of land across from Disneyland?" After all was said and done, Disney had purchased approximately 47 square miles of land, approximately twice the size of Manhattan.

The point is, when you meet with the potential seller, there is no reason for you to show up with your Rolex on, order the most expensive bottle of wine and toot your own horn about how successful you are in business. There may be a time for that, but during the first couple of meetings is not that time. Trust me, it will bump up the purchase price if they think you can afford more. I was working on a deal recently when the subject of how big the company doing the acquisition was came up over lunch. You could literally see the eyes of the seller get bigger and they started to be more aggressive in deal terms than they had been in the prior meetings. The seller even acknowledged it by saying "They are big enough, they can afford it.".

If you own a tract of land near the interstate and someone says they would like to buy it and gives you their business card showing they are a local CPA or attorney, you might come up with one price. If someone gives you their business card and they are Head of Land Acquisitions for McDonald's, I would venture to say your desired sales price would go up.

Key concepts to remember when valuing a company

Presuming you are acquiring a company with existing debt, remember that not all debt is created equal.

A few years ago, our team acquired three companies in the same revenue range, but two were very different in the details.

For simplicity sake, see below and think about which company you would rather purchase (assume all else being equal):

1. $20 million in sales, $ 2 million in debt owed to majority shareholder via shareholder loans
2. $20 million in sales, $ 1.9 million in debt owed to 19 different vendors at about $100,000 each

Obviously the details are where you will find out the hidden gems in this scenario. Presuming all else being equal, I would rather deal with the $2 million in debt with 1 lender, even though it is more debt, that dealing with 19 different vendors.

There are two schools of thought:

1 debt to 1 person - this is usually much easier to manage. However, from experience, this depends on the person:

- Are they involved in the business?
- What are the debt payment terms?
- What can they do if debt payments are missed?
- What other sources of income do they have? In other words, are they counting on this for the first of every month to survive?

19 debts to 19 different vendors - there are situations when this is easier to manage. For example, if you are trying to negotiate the debt and they realize they are not the only vendor. However, this is also very risky as it just takes 1 of those 19 vendors to get upset and file a lawsuit, which could then snowball lawsuits from others.

The end of this chapter is similar to the beginning. What is valuable to you may not be valuable to the seller. Use the standard industry multiples as a guide so you know from what position you will be negotiating, but remember that you are likely doing the acquisition because you have a long term goal in mind. This is not about buying a $250,000 house for $240,000 so you can flip it for $260,000. This is about buying a business that you can significantly improve, potentially bolt on to what you already have, and grow your whole company.

The seller will usually have a handful of variables they are looking at in your offer (price / terms / how their employees will be handled). However, you will (or should) have a dozen potential variables of your own as to why you are making the offer. In my experience, most of the time it is easier to give the seller the 'win' by giving them the value that they want while you get the terms you want on how you will pay. As a friend and client of mine says, "Your price, my terms."

NOTE TO REMEMBER: The majority of baby boomers, when they are selling their business, may not be doing so out of financial necessity for themselves, but for out of a desire and pride for continuation of their company (their legacy). THAT is what you are selling them.

You are not always selling them the money, you are selling them the continuation of their legacy, moving them into an advisory board role for your company and possibly an industry position, letting them focus their time as a visionary with the ability to increase their take home through cross selling of services / products to their customer base, removing them from the majority of the administrative functions that most of the entrepreneurs can't stand having to deal with right now. Also remind them that you are looking to buy other companies in the area and that if they help you find them (they likely know ALL the people their age looking to sell) they will participate in that revenue, and most importantly shift the risk from them to your company. That is what you are selling them. Oh and yes, sometimes you are selling them the way out that they have been looking for.

CHAPTER 12

Answers to Challenges You May Hear

Here are some challenges you should expect to hear and some possible responses. You should anticipate all of these objections at some point in the process and be prepared for them.

Psychology tells us that objections usually come from fear.

We fear the unknown.

How many of these objections can be overcome when they trust you will do what you say? Do you have a record of doing what you say you will do? Do you have a reputation in the city or industry which will be harmed if you screw them over? Do you have a vision for your company and will their company fit into that vision?

Figure out what they are really saying. Is it fear driving the objection? Maybe they honestly do not understand your proposal. If they are unable to verbalize and explain to their spouse or family or friends what they are doing with their business, then they do not understand it well enough and you will not likely get the deal done. You need to try again and do a better job of explaining why the deal is important for them.

Maybe they feel they can get a better deal elsewhere. Maybe they do not believe the proposal you are giving them. Again, this goes back to trust.

You might be talking with an owner who says they understand the finances for their business, BUT it might be how the numbers affect them as an individual, not as a business, and that is not the same thing. They may look at their personal tax return or personal financial statements and see a butterfly, but when you look at them, they are stretching out vendors to increase their personal cash flow, so you see a caterpillar. While they both likely have the same DNA, you are obviously looking at two different things.

Remember, the seller is the combination of your sales pitch to everyone you deal with.

- To the <u>potential</u> employees about why they should <u>come</u> work for you
- To the <u>existing</u> employees about why they should <u>stay</u> working for you
- To the <u>potential</u> customers about why they should <u>choose</u> your company
- To the <u>existing</u> customers about why they should <u>not leave</u> your company
- To your banker, your attorney, your accountant, etc.

You are pitching you and your business, the vision, your values, your future. Think through what you are going to say. Try explaining it to a child and ask them to tell you back, "What is it that I do?" Is it too complicated? This task is for more than just acquiring a company.

You should explain what is presumed in the expectations. In one acquisition we completed we were able to promise a payout to the selling shareholders over a period of three years. This was 100% contingent on the company meeting the projections one of the shareholders said the company could do based on already booked work. Fast forward two years into the transaction and the payout had to be adjusted to closer to five years. One of the selling shareholders got upset and said she felt she was misled, but when we showed how she had represented a certain level of performance and that we had done our part, everyone realized the disconnect. A formula based summary of this is:

> Reality
> - Vision
> - Goal
> - Expectation
> Happy (unhappy)

If the parties receive at or more than they expected / envisioned or had a goal for, then they are happy. If they don't, then they are unhappy. There is nothing that says the expectations and vision can't shift along the way. Sometimes it will shift up and sometimes it will shift down.

> Reality: Receive $900,000
> - Expectation of $1,000,000
> Result: ($100,000) shortfall = unhappy

Objection # 1: I had lunch with an adviser who says I should ask for _____ (insert one of many possible things, such as more money up front, higher value, more collateral, higher interest rate, etc.).

One day you will be driving to the office, thinking about how well the meeting went with the seller on the previous Friday.

When you get to your desk, you will get an email. Turns out the seller received an email from a friend of theirs who had, in the past, served as an adviser (or attorney or accountant or one of a dozen different roles) years ago, and the seller had lunch with them over the weekend.

The 'adviser' will no doubt think that the seller needs to ask for:

> – more money up front, or
> – larger % of the new business, or
> – more security, or

- they 'know a guy' who may be interested in buying the business instead.

Despite the fact this is a pain in the butt, it is actually good. This way you will win over the adviser and never have an issue down the road with the seller second guessing you. You don't want seller's remorse during the transition period, or the 'adviser' in an "I told you so" role. You also don't want to throw their adviser under the bus or speak ill of them, as that type of negative talk will never play itself out well in the long run.

In one of my largest acquisitions, the seller actually went back to a "grass is greener" offer, which for them was a private equity firm. They worked through details with them for two months, and then came back to me when they realized they would actually get more money and value over time with the deal I had presented. The private equity firm had offered longer payout terms, earn outs, and work requirements. My offer had fewer psychological handcuffs.

You could also say, "I realize you would get a 4.0x EBITDA multiple if you went with a private equity firm, but, how long of an employment contract will they require you to sign, what claw back terms and what are the other details you are agreeing to? In our transaction, we are giving you a 6x EBITDA multiple, which is 150% of what they are offering. Sure we will pay it over time, but you also have the upside potential to make more with us."

You will benefit when you show them the upside potential. If they are making more, you are making more, so what do you care? They deserve to make more if they help grow it more.

Objection # 2: I feel I may be selling too soon.

He or she has a fear of selling too soon. This may be driven more by not knowing what they want to do when they sell. Is the industry changing? How is the economy as a whole?

There is no need to pressure people into selling. If they want to hold out and deal with the minutia for another six months, then let them. Keep the conversation flowing and stay in contact with them, but do not pressure them to sell.

Sometimes they just need to talk about their fears and then think about them. Focus on the things they will no longer have to deal with when they sell. "That's true, I do not want you selling if you aren't ready, I just see the benefits for us if we do the acquisition and I see you not having to deal with the day to day administrative task. You can always keep working in the industry and participate in the upside through new business, but you won't have to deal with the administrative functions you mentioned last time we spoke."

A client made what I thought was an overly generous offer to a company for what would have been a strategic fit for both of them. They went back and forth for months and months, with the target company repeating they thought they were selling too soon. My client set a deadline for an answer, but the seller couldn't make up their mind, so my client moved on with their business plan and focused on other acquisitions. Four months later they ran into each other at a function and closed on a deal together 30 days after that.

Objection # 3: What if I sell to you and then you sell to someone else within a year for more?

Valid concern. In Las Vegas, during roughly 2001 - 2007, you could put a deposit on a new construction home for $5,000. The home would be built over the next six months. Once construction was done, you as could list the house for sale, and within a month the price would have increased $30,000 - $70,000. By buying early you could flip the home and make a huge return. I know this to be true as I was one of those people. Similar to camping out for concert tickets in the 80's and 90's, people would literally be sleep in cars by empty lots waiting for the developers to 'release' the homes to the public.

The media had many questions about if the home builders were selling too soon, or if they could prevent buyers from flipping the properties. Some developers attempted to put in stipulations that buyers couldn't sell within 12 months of purchase. That worked in some cases, but not in all.

If the seller tells you that she is concerned you are just going to flip the property, you'll have to decide how to proceed. First you should ask yourself if you are planning on selling the entire company in a short period. If not, then you have nothing to worry about. If there is a chance, you can mitigate this by adding in provisions which would allow you to do so.

You can tell the seller, "If we sell within the next 12 months for more than the purchase price, you will get ___% of the gain over and above what we paid." Whether that percent is 5% or 50% is up to you.

This is one of those areas which in my opinion should not represent a major negotiation point (unless of course you plan to flip the company within 12 months). Sometimes it's best to let the seller feel they 'won' this point by agreeing that if you sell within 12 months, they have right of first refusal.

The alternative is to just tell them that if you sell within two days or two years of the purchase, they do not get any of the upside. They can't have their cake and eat it too. If they sell to you, it is yours, and you should not be restricted on what you can or can't do with your purchase.

Objection # 4: I am not selling for enough.

You should determine what enough is. "When you say enough, are you saying you want a higher purchase price or you want to get more of a percentage of the new business we get in the next 12 months?"

Figure out what they are asking for.

"I can see your point, but I feel if we commit to too much now, without seeing how many of the customers will stay with us or if the employees will stay, we are not going to be sharing in the risk fairly."

Now is the time to lay out the burden of the risk. If you are asking them to take a larger seller note or finance the entire thing, do not sound like a spoiled child, but do point out the fact of the unknowns on your end. Remember, they are going to presume ALL employees will want to work for you and ALL customers will stay, so if neither of those are realistic expectations it is more than OK for you to point that out the seller. This is not a risk free transaction for you and your company, regardless of how little the seller may feel you are investing up front.

Find out what they mean when they say they are not selling for enough. If they feel they are missing out on the upside, see if there is a commission plan where they can participate for a fixed period of time in that growth, if (and only if) they do specific tasks to assist in achieving those goals.

Objection # 5: I want more cash up front.

Valid concern. You need to gauge why they need more cash up front. Is there a fear they will not get the next payment, or is there a pending need which requires them to get more cash up front?

You should also determine what "up front" means. For some sellers it means the day they sign the paperwork, for others it means within 90 days of signing. Depending on the time of year, they may want to postpone receiving some of their down payment until after December 31, so they can push off the tax bill another 12 months. Usually if you are closing during the 4th quarter (October / November / December) there will be some flexibility in this as well.

Is the cash they are getting contingent on you getting the money from a 3rd party based on their financial statements? Find out from that 3rd party what the time frame is and relay that to the seller and ALWAYS keep the communication flow very fluid so they know what is going on with the timing.

Be honest in what you can and cannot do. If they want $1 million at closing and you cannot give them that, say so. But say, "I realize you want to get about $1 million up front, but we just do not have the liquidity for that. However, based on conversations with our bankers and the existing cash flow of the business, I feel comfortable we will be able to get the $ 1 million to you within the first 90 - 120 days." Again, if there are limitations or factors outside of your control, this is the time to state it. These conversations are sales conversations. They want a feature (more cash up front) that your product (your offer) can't do, but explain to them why they product you are selling them gets them what they need.

If they still push back and say they want more cash up front, it is perfectly fair to remind them that if they start the process all over with a new potential buyer, by the time they come to terms with them and are ready to close, you will have already passed the 90-120 day mark you have said you would deliver on the $1 million.

Objection # 6: I want more security and collateral.

Their concern here is in your ability to pay and what happens if you do not pay or if the business does poorly. The last thing they want to do is come back and have to run the business again to fix what you have messed up.

Ask them what kind of security and collateral they would prefer. They may not know the answer as they honestly expected you to balk at the question.

Do you have additional collateral you can put up?

I would not suggest doing a personal guarantee unless you have to. If and when the issue is raised, be prepared to discuss this. You are not saying no to a personal guarantee because you do not believe it in, but you are already 100% into the company with what you are doing with your business and your family.

For many people, personal guarantees are deal breakers (and in many cases they should be).

If you do agree to a personal guarantee, I would suggest you do it for a set period of time and/or have it released when a certain percentage has been paid.

You can explain that by doing a personal guarantee it will restrict some of the plans and growth for you and the company for the future. The reality is that is true. If you have partners, it is not fair for one partner to be the only personal guarantee. If you are a solo owner now and down the road you want to merge with someone, then all of a sudden you are personal guarantee on it and they are not.

If they have brought it up, expect push back as you likely have a personal guarantee on a bank loan or car loan. But in this instance, decide if you are comfortable with it. Consider personal preference, size of the loan, and duration of the loan or the guarantee, among the other factors.

Giving them security over the assets of the company until their loan is paid off should not be an issue. Your goals are the same, you want to use those assets to generate cash to pay down the loan.

Objection # 7: What about my employees? What about the brand I created?

You should expect this question early in the process.

You should already know what you want to do with their employees.

- Do you want to keep them?
- Do you NEED to keep them for transition?
- Do you want them terminated the day of the acquisition? (For unemployment tax purposes you likely do not want to bring over employees which you know you will be terminating in the coming months.)

If you do not want to keep the employees, remember these are people with their own lives, so treat them properly. Work with the seller on a severance package, or call around to try and help find them work. If there are a lot of people, hire a company to do this for you.

I have only seen it beneficial to keep the existing company brand in place in a few select situations. More often than not it is necessary to make all companies operate under one name. ***Be honest with yourself and others,*** *maybe you want to adopt their name versus keeping your company name.* If they have been around for longer than you have, taking on their name might be better. There could also be a benefit to you as an individual if you purchase them, but have the company name changed to theirs. If your company had a hiccup you want to get rid of, this could be the chance. There should be no ego in this process. Do what is best for the company and all of the employees / customers / owners / vendors.

Objection # 8: I am not ready to sell yet.

This is a legitimate objection. If they are not ready to sell yet, then you do not want to waste your time or their time. HOWEVER, make sure that is the real reason and it's not a different objection masked as them not telling you what is really going on in their head.

Dan Kennedy is a marketing strategist. In his 2010 book *Making Them Believe* he says, "The only difference between salad and garbage is timing." This quote has been credited to many speakers, but the point is clear. If they aren't ready to sell, they aren't ready.

True timing issues can sometimes be overcome.

You need to determine if they are not ready to sell, or if they do not know what they will do with their life without their company to run. Parents get empty nest syndrome when their kids go to college after being at home for 18 years. Owners who have been in business for 15, 20 or 25 years can have that same sense of loss.

If they aren't ready to sell and there is no strategic benefit to doing a joint venture, then thank them for their time, keep in touch, and move on to your next acquisition target.

Objection # 9: If I stay as an owner and do all those things, then my business will be worth more.

They may not believe the value which you and your team represent. It is your job to convince them of this.

Again, they may have a caterpillar and they believe it will be a butterfly sometime, but in reality only about 10% of caterpillars turn into butterflies; the rest die, are eaten by birds, or die of disease. They may believe they can make that leap, and maybe they can, but the issue is, are they ready to move on to do something else, today? And are they ready to carry with it the risk of them not achieving that goal?

"Yes, that is possible, but we started talking about this transaction so you would be able to do other things in your life besides this business. You had said you wanted to _____ (travel more, save on taxes, not deal with the day to day) instead of work in the business 60 hours a week?"

If they push in this direction, remember you can always propose a joint venture with them. You can manage the administrative part of the business (or even the manufacturing side) and they phase out slowly. This will allow them to participate in the upside, but just not have the 60 hour work weeks. In this situation; however, you would be looking down the road to lock in a potential purchase, option or right of first refusal.

Objection # 10: I do not want an earn out? I don't want you lowering the price down the road for something you should have prevented?

An earn out is a situation such as $100,000 now and 15% of sales for the next 5 years.

An installment sale is, for example, $10,000 a month for 60 months.

It is important to make the distinction and make sure you (and they) know which one you are proposing. If you are expecting them to take a risk on getting paid, you should take the risk of maintaining the business.

All else being equal, in the above examples, the seller should be able to earn more money during the earn out as they are carrying some of the risk of it being less if you do not perform. Ideally you can create a scenario where you don't care which one they pick, as then, they are choosing from two options you present, but they feel it is their choice.

Regardless of how it is set up, the payment terms should be lined out and the calculation pre-determined. If you say 50% of EBITDA, but then give yourself a 200% salary increase, you might never have any EBITDA.

If you say 50% of EBITDA, which is defined as Sales minus Cost of Goods sold minus Overhead of no more than __% and Admin costs of ___% of sales, then that is something that can be used to calculate an expected payment.

It makes sense for you to use their historical numbers to calculate this. This is something you should know as well, so it is an exercise well worth the time.

Think to yourself, "If I wanted to screw them over, how would I do it?" Then you need to remove that risk from the calculation, even to the point of explicitly stating it in the documents. You can say, "In the calculation of payment, compensation expenses can never be more than __% of sales."

Trust me, they are thinking, "If they wanted to screw me over, how would they do it," so you need to be prepared to answer it and if you can answer it before they ask it to you, that should build up trust.

<u>Objection # 11: Why should I have to take a risk that you will manage the customers properly?</u>

Great question. They shouldn't! Here is where you get to talk about how good you are with your customers and how long they have been with you.

You can de-risk this fear by explaining what you do to mitigate customer complaints. Everyone gets customer complaints. Their fear in this case is you will not manage their customers. It is like a job interview, now is your time to tell them what you do already to manage customers and keep them happy.

"Mario, that's a great question. I am not expecting you too. I am going to need your help in the transition process and to monitor the customer satisfaction surveys we get on every transaction. We use Net Promoter

Score®, and historically we receive over an 8.5 - 9.5 out of 10 from our customers. If we dip below the 8.5 mark, our management team receives an email notification and we have the manager call the customer within 4 hours to resolve it. So the short answer is you will have to trust us in this process. You are familiar with our company and our brand, but I just wanted to show you how much we value the management of customer expectations."

John Lydgate was a monk and poet who died in 1451. One of Lydgate's poems was adapted and used frequently by Abraham Lincoln. "You can please all of the people some of the time and some of the people all of the time, but you can't please all of the people all of the time." Do not tell the seller all of your customers are happy. If you believe that then you likely do not know all of your customers well enough. Unfortunately there are some that are not happy, even if it's a small percentage.

This is where you explain what you do to make them happy, keep them happy, and, most importantly, when they are unhappy, what you do to make things rights.

Objection #12: I don't want to sign a non-compete.

For me this raises a red flag. Are you selling the business because you want out, or are you selling the business with plans to open up again in 12 months and steal customers and employees?

As long as there are payments still being made (and potentially for some period after) there should be no reason why a non-compete would be objected to. They either want to sell and get out or they don't.

If they do not want to sign a non-compete, ask them why? If they change their mind and want to jump back in, why wouldn't they joint venture with you in the industry. This would be another opportunity for you to handle the administrative tasks of running the business for a fee and they focus on sales. But getting the seller to sign a non-compete, even if for only 12-24 months, is not out of line.

NOTE: Depending on your state, non-compete agreements may be unenforceable in regards to your industry, but you should be able to prevent them going after a specific list of customers / employees for a period of time. That is really what you are looking to prevent. Some states actually only honor non-competes for owners selling. Just make sure you aren't asking them to sign something that for all intent and purposes will be negated later on by a court.

<u>Objection #13: I don't want to have to subordinate to other debtors down the road and I don't think you can assure me of that.</u>

Subordinated debt - meaning even if a company owes you money, they owe it to someone else first. Look at this as a 2nd mortgage or a line of credit on your home. The 1st mortgage is, well just that, 1st in line.

Let's say you buy the business from Brent. Brent gets his monthly or quarterly payments.

Now your business draws on its line of credit. You start increasing your overhead faster than you should.

Now you fall behind with your creditors. All the while Brent is getting his payments and is oblivious to what's going on in the business.

Maybe you get in a situation where you have to go get a bank loan to catch up on creditors and vendors and refinance to a lower monthly payment. The bank says, "We will do the deal, however, we don't know Brent, nor do we care if he gets his payments. We want Brent to agree to subordinate to us and we have to approve payments to him." What this means is the bank can tell you if you are not hitting certain ratios or milestones, they can prevent you from making payments on other debtors.

So you have to go to Brent and renegotiate and ask him to subordinate to the bank.

Brent is going to say, "That's not my problem, I want my payments on time."

The bank is going to say, "If Brent doesn't subordinate, we won't give you the money and your business may go under and Brent won't get anything."

Those are legitimate concerns and I have seen this happen.

The key to avoiding this is managing the cash flow and performance metrics in advance so you never get to this point.

In regards to this objection and how you get over it, it could include:

- Creating a sinking fund or escrow account where you prepay into it some amount that is owed to the seller, but not released.
- Accelerations clauses that say if certain financial metrics are not met then the seller gets more money faster
- Restrictions on larger purchases / transactions which could potentially get the buyer into a situation like this. For example, if you do another acquisitions within the first 12 months subsequent to this purchase, the monthly payments increase 50%.
- Require payouts of a certain amount of funds that are raised. For example, if the company borrows more than $500,000 in any 12 month period, then an additional payment of $100,000 will have to be made on the balance owed.

Objection # 14: I want you to buy the building as well. OR, I don't want you to buy the building, but want you to rent out the office.

This objection has been a deal breaker on more than one occasion. There was a company outside of Chicago we were speaking with that did about $15 million in revenue and we were going to get a great deal on it. The problem was, they owned their office / warehouse. That in and of itself wasn't a huge problem, but it did not fit within our company model and we didn't need or want to have a building. The goal was to use that company more for sales and less for production or administration. The real estate market in that area did not allow for them to sell the building easily so despite the fact that the business transaction was great for both parties, the building soured the deal.

We had another situation when we were growing our CPA practice through acquisitions. We had multiple offices in Las Vegas and we met with another CPA we had known for years. Super talented woman, but at the end of the meeting she brought up the fact she owned her building. Well we owned our building and had just done a transaction with another firm in town which owned their building, so having three locations on that side of town was not a good idea. This also happened to be when real estate prices in Las Vegas were depressed, so selling her building wasn't a viable option and the deal pretty much ended right then and there. The numbers on the deal made sense for us, but buying (or renting) her building eliminated all those potential savings.

However, there are certainly opportunities when buying a building is a great strategy. For the business outside of Chicago, we had actually looked into purchasing the building through a bank loan (so the seller gets money out immediately), and the balance on the business would be in installments. From a financing point of view it made sense. That would have been a win for the seller and for us. However, as mentioned above, having a building there was not part of our overall strategy.

SIDE NOTE: Let this be a reminder to you if you are contemplating buying your own building or if you own your own building. At some point if you want to sell your business, the buyer more than likely will not want the building as well, then you will be stuck with an empty building.

The above should encompass the majority of questions or challenges you might hear. If you hear others, please feel free to email me and I will either respond directly to you or address my responses in an article.

CHAPTER 13

Tax and Legal Considerations

During the years 1979 - 1998, the *Choose Your Own Adventure* series was one the most popular children's book series, ranking 4th on the all-time best-seller list with over 260 million copies sold. For those of you who grew up in that time and lived in a box, the title pretty much says it all. The book was laid out so that the reader could determine which way to go on their adventure. You were the spy or the private investigator or the race car driver or whatever. You would read a couple pages and determine which path to go. If you wanted to go into the cave, you turned to page 75. If you wanted to climb over the cave to the top of the waterfall, you turned to page 84. And when you got to that page, the story continued.

Taxes and legal structure are like a *Choose Your Own Adventure* book.

- If you want to acquire with all debt through your C corporation, that is one adventure.
- If you want to exchange shares of your larger company for shares in their smaller company, that is another adventure.
- If you want the seller to finance the transaction and pay them interest on top of the debt they are self-financing, that is another adventure.

There is an endless supply of potential ways to structure it.

It depends on what YOU want to do and what the seller wants, or sometimes needs, to do.

To be clear, there is no way to cover all the potential issues in just one chapter. This will likely be the shortest chapter in the book as we are not making claims or representations of how to structure your transaction in terms of how it will affect your (or the seller's) tax situation.

There are many books that cover this topic, and many more online sources with details for your specific situation. You should also consult with your advisers.

As entrepreneurs and business owners, once you lay out the goal of your transaction, the high level terms on which you agree, a good attorney should be able to draw up the documents for you.

If you are meeting with attorneys who are constantly telling you why something will not work, be very concerned. During one of our larger transactions, the attorney for one of the parties responded to all our ideas with, "No that doesn't work," without giving us any help or suggestions on how to make it work. You need an adviser who has an entrepreneurial mind, who will say, "Ok, I see what you want to do. Are we able to do this? Yes, if we structure it this way…"

Legal Considerations

There were acquisitions we did without formal legal counsel for either side. There were also acquisitions for which both sides used legal counsel.

Unless you have done this before, I would strongly recommend hiring an attorney to review the final documents or at a minimum taking an attorney friend to lunch to get some key points. (They will likely also suggest both sides get legal counsel to review.)

Things to think about:

How do things split up if the transaction fails?

What happens if the Seller does not live up to their end of the bargain? Is there a claw-back of any money paid during the negotiations?

What remedies will the seller want if you do not live up to your end of the bargain?

You have to remember, you are bringing a partner to your business. That 'partner' might not be an equity partner or an income partner, but you are letting someone else bring their culture, customers, employees and their history (good and bad) into your world.

When you bring on a new customer, you have a certain amount of risk. You have hopefully researched them or reached out to them. There is only so much damage one client can do right? (Wrong, but that is a different discussion.) But if you are bringing over 300 or even 3,000 customers from the seller's company, you need to make sure you cover your bases. Are you assuming some warranties that the seller made in prior years?

Some people prefer that you acquire the entity and some people prefer you acquire the assets. As discussed in earlier chapters, the latter is usually the preferred approach so you do not have to worry about skeletons in the closet of the entity. However, due to software licensing or industry requirements you might need to take over the history of the company so you can say, "We have been around for over 20 years."

One of the first entities my partner and I took over turned out to have three years of back payroll taxes which we had to fight with the IRS about. We eventually won, but he and I spent a lot of time, money and sleepless nights pondering how to handle a situation we were unaware of as we inherited it through a subsidiary.

Along with due diligence, I strongly encourage you to address tax and legal considerations with outside advisers, CPAs, attorneys, or people with experience in this field. Much of the time we had to come up with creative ideas on how to get a deal structured, but we still needed third party advisers to validate our ideas and tell us what would be the most beneficial tax and legal structure. Those types of reassurances will help the seller sleep at night and will be money well spent.

Concurrent with finalizing the business structure, it is wise to consult with your tax adviser on the allocation of purchase price to the assets being purchased. This could be hugely beneficial to you as the buyer and it could also be painfully detrimental to the seller if not done right. The allocation of purchase price will be instrumental in determining tax deductions for your company on a go forward basis.

PART THREE

REPEAT

Completing the first transaction is only the beginning.

It is important for you to spend the time needed to integrate the transaction with your existing business and cultivate your customers. You likely already spend a lot of time making sure new employees and customers are happy, and if you have just completed and acquisition (or merger), you now have many more employees and customers to satisfy.

Remember: Just as sellers have personality issues, so do employees and customers. You need to mitigate any fears they have about their new employer or new vendor relationships.

I would be remiss if I claimed that this process is 'easy.' There are few things in life that are 'easy,' but the more you practice them, the better you get.

Malcolm Gladwell, in his 2008 book *Outliers,* referenced the now well known '10,000 hour rule.' This 'rule' is based on research done by Anders Ericsson. In their 2016 book *Peak*, Anders Ericsson and Robert Pool discuss what it takes to truly become an expert, and explain how the 10,000 hours are not an absolute and how there are better ways. *Peak* condenses three decades of research about the process and about how to get into the proper mental state to focus on what you are building and want you want to be. In developing your own acquisition strategy, you will find that when you are beginning, the learning curve will be steep. But with the knowledge you will gain, you will become more and more proficient.

Now that your first acquisition is complete, there are some steps you need to take to make sure (1) that it is a success, (2) that your foundation is prepared for the next one, and then (3) that you repeat the process to acquire your 2nd and 3rd and 4th businesses.

Let's focus on what happens immediately after you announce the transaction. Literally minutes after.

Scenario: You are invited to a local meeting of entrepreneurs and the leader is going around the table having the guests introduce themselves. Everyone has impressive businesses, and has grown them from start up to their current level. One person says, "We were founded in ____ and have been growing for a while now. We recently held a strategy session to map out the next three to five years and put an acquisitions strategy in place. We just completed our first acquisition, which should increase our revenues by 60% over what we did last year, and we intend on doing another acquisition in the early part of next year."

Now just hearing that, with no other information, you will view that entrepreneur differently than anyone else in the room. PLEASE note, I am not saying you want to buy your competitors because you want random people at lunches to look at you in a different light. My point is that they will look at you in a different light and hold you to a different standard. You have taken a risk which most companies do not take. You have more at stake. You have more challenges. You have different/new experiences which they may not have. Does that mean you are braver or smarter or richer or crazier? Who knows? But regardless, people will look at you differently and expect more from you. Any potential sellers in the room will likely seek you out before they leave as well.

When you tell your customers you just acquired another company, they will presume (correctly or not) that you are a larger company. If you manage the transaction and the integration correctly, it will provide tremendous intangible benefits to your existing business.

Here is an example of an email that could be sent out by a law firm after they complete an acquisition.

We are pleased to share some very exciting news. LAW FIRM ONE will be combining with the well-respected national law firm LAW FIRM 2.

This is a significant step in LAW FIRM ONE'S continuing strategic growth. LAW FIRM TWO, which has more than ____ attorneys in offices in City 1, City 2 and City 3, is well regarded as a national law firm with prominent practices in service 1, service 2, litigation, business, and finance, which are an excellent complement to LAW FIRM ONE'S strengths. This is a great cultural fit as well, given our firms' shared commitments to our clients, diversity, pro bono service and community involvement.

We anticipate this combination will be effective January 1, 2017. The combined firm, which will maintain the name of LAW FIRM ONE, will rank among the 100 largest law firms in the country, with more than _____ attorneys and advisors across __ offices in _____ states as well as Washington, D.C.

We're very excited to have this opportunity to join with such a highly respected law firm. We look forward to the opportunity to introduce you to our new colleagues in the near future. Until then, we encourage you to learn more about LAW FIRM TWO by visiting its website: http://www._____

Thank you for the trust you continue to place in us.

Now I have no idea if Law Firm Two is good or bad. I do not do business in any of the cities or industries that Law Firm Two does business in, either. However it does give me a good feeling to know that the firm I have referred many clients to, as well has have personally used, has a growth strategy vs a status quo strategy. It will matter to customers. It will matter to employees. It will matter to vendors. Please do not underestimate how much it will matter.

NOTE: Do not get caught up in the rewards and miss the risks. It goes both ways. An acquisition will create some fear among employees, most likely those who are not sure if they are A players and will make the cut.

I have never seen A players get upset over acquisitions as the majority of the time it gives them more products to sell, more upside and / or more challenge to be the best.

Now let's focus on repeating the process and making the acquisition successful.

CHAPTER 14

Transition Team/Culture Effect

In October 2016, *Fortune* magazine posted an article on its website titled *Japan's Aging Population Has Business Owners Struggling to Find Successors.* The article states that according to Tokyo Shoko Research, 26,700 companies shut down voluntarily (not through bankruptcy) as the owners were unable to find suitable successors or faced a dim business outlook due to their aging owners.

Presidents Elect have a transition team.

Family businesses have a transition team for transferring power.

Many colleges have a 'transition team' for incoming freshmen.

When doing an acquisition, you need to have a transition team.

A transition team does not mean you send an email and say, "Please let me know if you have questions, we are excited to have you here." A transition team does not mean sending out an 800 number for people to call with questions.

The dictionary defines the word "transition" as *'movement, passage, or change from one position, state, stage, subject, concept, etc., to another; change.'*

Having a transition team means having specific people whose job it is to ensure that new employees are welcome. When you hire a new person, you should have at least one person at the company who is charged with making sure they settle in and are comfortable.

In their 2009 Bain & Company article, *10 Steps to a Successful M&A Integration,* authors Ted Rouse and Tory Frame discuss how the loss of key people is one of the top three areas most companies fail to perform in post transaction integration, the other two being (1) missing targets and timelines on the integration plan, and (2) poor performance in the core business because of distractions.

The purpose of the transition team is to allow you and the other executives to focus on growing the business and allowing the key people in the company being acquired to be focused and comfortable in their new situation.

The purpose of the transition team is to keep all the little items from falling through the cracks.

Some examples of things that may appear small, but can create cracks in the foundation of an attractive acquisition.

Example when XYZ is the buyer of ABC

- XYZ has an annual family picnic and ABC staff usually have their own games at the picnic and wonder 'can our games get integrated in to the XYZ picnic'
- XYZ has different holiday schedules than ABC
- XYZ starts 30 minutes earlier in their day than ABC and some of ABC's workers will have to drastically change their child care times based on this change
- Dress code differences between both companies
- Smoke break policies between both companies
- ABC used to buy lunch for the whole department and have cake in the break room on people's birthdays and XYZ just doesn't do that

I am certainly not saying that you as the buyer have to personally handle all of these scenarios, but you should have someone on your staff who is charged with making sure these are addressed so the new employees do not feel they are forced into a job they never would have applied for.

I have seen these scenarios and even to the point of one done in a 4th quarter of the year where the ABC team had their own "Christmas Party" with just their families as they didn't feel accepted in the XYZ one.

Your transition team can also be your culture team. The culture team is the one charged with making sure the cultures of the two companies are explained / defined / blended and questions answered.

Your culture team finds out who are the key people on the ABC side and work with them. No matter how big or small the companies are, there are always a handful of people who unofficially represent that masses. Those are the ones everyone will watch to see if things are alright. If they are happy, then usually the rest of the team will be happy.

<u>Buddy system</u> - With smaller firms this works well. Have each person on the transition team have three - five 'buddies' they check in with once every week or two for the first 90 days to make sure all is going smoothly with no questions, or answering questions they do have. Make sure you to define what they have the ability to commit to, and what someone else has a say in answering. You are not trying to create red tape, but for the new employees, they will take whatever they are told as 'company policy,' so you want to make sure the transition team knows what they are talking about.

For larger companies, different divisions may have their own transition teams.

For really large companies, you could have a team that serves as a dedicated transition team going from acquisition to acquisition.

Transition teams should meet about once a week to review challenges or areas of concern they are seeing.

The team should be there for the orientation when the acquisition is announced.

They should have a monthly budget to spend on group events to intermingle the two companies. They should be given autonomy to use the budget as they see fit. Whether it is Food Trucks being brought to the parking lot, or happy hour, or a softball prize, or even a family picnic, the sooner the two companies can feel connected the sooner people can start focusing on the business.

Culture changes

Just as you have been telling your staff for years, as the company grows, there may be changes for you as well. You need to be prepared for culture changes that will occur with new people.

Maybe you started this process with a defined Mission, Vision and Values for your company. With this growth and influx of new people, customers, and their values, has any part of your company changed? Is it time to revisit and define new goals or recognize a new focus?

You should have your 'culture team' be prepared for mutiny in the ranks.

We held a human resources meeting with about 20 people a week after a transaction. I thought a fight was going to break out over the fact that the employees of the company we bought did not get to roll their vacation time over into our plan. After about 15 minutes of 'this is what we had' and 'our plan was better,' we found out that for the 20 people in the room, only two of them were actually affected by more than $250 (the others thought they would be affected, but they really weren't). We talked with those two and found out 'why' they were so affected, and it had to do with vacation time based on when their kids were out of school and other family events they planned every year. We got the whole thing settled, but this was something we could have prepared better for. Many of these are hard to anticipate, though, as you do not always know what practices the employees of the acquisition company will feel are unfair.

A great exercise is to have your transition team hold a mock presentation to some of your more outspoken existing employees. Ask those employees to step into the role of a new employee who was just acquired. Ask them to be as negative as possible and throw any question at your transition team they can think of. You will be surprised to hear some of the questions. This will really prepare you for rolling out the integration team to the company being acquired, and will give you great insight into areas of your company which you may not know are lacking.

CHAPTER 15

FAQS for Employees/ Vendors/Customers

Communication is the key to many areas of business and life. This chapter discusses some of the ways to help communicate what is happening to your company, your vendors and your customers.

When you are not communicating, that does not mean the conversations have stopped. That does not mean people are not asking questions and coming up with their own solution / answer / idea / scenario.

Prior to the closing of the acquisition, you should have specific FAQ's that are given to all employees of both companies that explain what is happening. 90% of the people in the room will be listening to your announcement and thinking, "How will this affect me?" The other 10% are not really listening to you, anyway, because their mind is elsewhere.

As the closing date gets nearer, the number of people who will be told (or hear) about the acquisition will increase, and more and more will have to be told. Obviously, some of this depends on how are you set up (i.e. public company, private company, closely held, multiple offices) and your industry. If you are buying from someone who is retiring in 6 months, they may not want that piece of information leaking out. Frankly, neither do you; you want to be able to control the story.

You want to insure that the people who find out keep their mouths shut. We had just completed a very large acquisition and were in talks (final stages of documents, actually) for another large acquisition and almost had a major issue. One of our employees was at an industry conference, and opened up his mouth about a pending acquisition. The person he was speaking with was smart enough to figure out who the seller was based on the people sitting together at meals and talking. It was very embarrassing for the seller but luckily he talked through the issue and the transaction moved forward.

Here is a general idea of the order of how the information flow goes, working from the inside out.

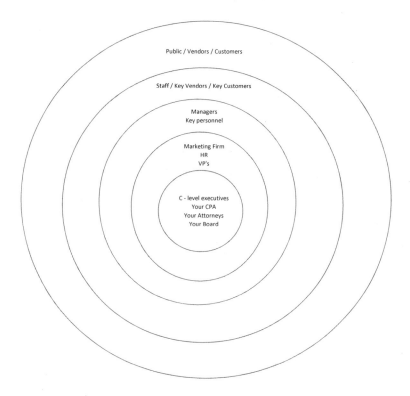

At one of the companies we did this with, acquisitions were part of their three year plan, as well as in their Painted Picture and a regularly occurrence, so it was not much of a surprise when a new one was done.

For your company it might be different. But regardless, you want to be as prepared as possible for the company being bought, AND for your existing company employees to have questions. Do not presume only your employees will have questions or thinking "how does this affect me?".

Put yourself in their shoes.

If you are able to get it done (which I recommend), the day of announcement, the employees of the company being bought should receive:

- New email address
- New business cards
- FAQ

Prior to the all company announcement, key members of the team should be told about it. These are the people who the other employees will look at and say, Well, if Steve is not freaking out, then I won't freak out." This notice can be given to them an hour or weeks before the general public is told. It is up to you how you want to let them know.

Marketing can be done based on your own timing, but you will want to have the branding sorted out and ready to go as soon as possible. If possible, post an announcement on the website of the company being bought.

If you are not changing the name, you can just say "XYZ Corp, an ABC Company."

The point is, once the announcement is made, the majority of your time will be (and should be) spent on talking with your employees, vendors, customers, and key partners.

This is one of those areas that you really cannot over do. It is unlikely anyone will complain, "They gave me too much information." And if they do, so be it.

Included in the exhibits are examples of some FAQs you should prepared and give to employees. Many things will not change, and you should tell them. But many things will change, and the timing will be up to you how quickly you roll out those changes.

For vendors, many of them will just want to know where to send the new invoices to for payment. Depending on the type of vendor, they may inquire about how they can get more business from you. Feel free to use this as an opportunity to say you are not sure what direction you will go, or that you would love to get them to do a proposal on all of the work. There is nothing wrong with using this to have the vendors sharpen their pencils and give you a new proposal. That is a large part of why you are doing the acquisition, so that you can save money based on scale.

For customers, I encourage you to provide them with a key contact at your company (or the seller's company). Explain what will change and what will not change. Ideally, very little will change from their point of view, except to make your service or delivery time or offerings better for them. No customer wants to hear how great things are going for you and your expansion, only to then hear that even though you used to offer them 45 day terms, because of the acquisition you now have to get paid in 30 days.

The company that mows the lawn for many houses in our neighborhood recently was sold. Everyone received a letter in the mail saying it had taken place. That was it. Nothing personal, no phone call or email. What happened over the coming months was of no surprise to me. People started to shop around. There was no loyalty to the new owners because "we didn't select them". A simple phone call from the Seller and/or introduction call from the buyer to say "Is there anything specific we should be looking for or focusing on when we come to your house?" would have solved many of their transition issues.

CHAPTER 16

Integration (What Happens Day 2)

Day 1: Acquisition completed, congratulations!
Day 2: Now what do we do?

So much energy has gone into this transaction, and you have spent a tremendous amount of time getting all the parties on the same page.

Unfortunately, NOW is when the heavy lifting starts. NOW is when the hard decisions have to be made (ideally some of them were made concurrent with the closing).

We have discussed integrating cultures and keeping the employees happy. Just as business owners are, on average, an aging population, so is the workforce. Thus, your integration plan has to account for your employees and whichever of their employees you are taking on in this transaction.

It is also important to not lose sight of the customers.

The Parthenon is an ancient temple in Athens, Greece. You have likely seen the image. The massive pillars hold up the huge stone roof. It is a significant tourist attraction and one of the world's greatest cultural monuments. An acquisition is like the Parthenon. Each column of the temple is a specific area of the business holding up the roof. You have the employees and the culture. You have the financial piece. You have management. You have suppliers and vendors. And of course you have customers.

Do not grow too fast for your customers

Rapid growth is one of the toughest challenges to sustain. There is a local breakfast place in Las Vegas where a wait of less than 30 minutes on the weekend would get you excited. That's just how long you have to wait. Aside from having very little competition in the area, the food is great, service is amazing and prices are reasonable. The restaurant had about 1,000 square feet of seating area, and when a neighboring tenant moved out, the landlord approached them about taking over the connecting space. They could work on the new space and, when ready, close one weekend, take down the dividing wall, and they would then have another 600+ square feet for tables. So they did. They even added a fresh juice station and did a much needed kitchen expansion. Fast forward. We ate there two months after the expansion. We only waited 15 minutes for a table, but then we were given a corner table in the back under the A/C so it was freezing. And while they did move us when we asked, the prior build out location didn't need the double A/C so no tables had that issue. 20 minutes later we ordered … and were there for two hours. Two hours. Each meal came out at a different time, and my wife's meal tasted completely different from the previous 10 times she had ordered it. Despite asking three times, my daughter never got her orange juice. My meal made me sick (literally… sick before we even left). I could go on and on. Over the last three years my wife and I had gone once a month for brunch after church, and now we would not go there even if the meal were free. Timing was off, food production wasn't there, too many wait staff crowded stations which caused delays. They were not prepared to handle the growth, and it killed them. I am sure you have seem something similar at restaurants or businesses you frequent.

Another example of growth not being handled well is Haggen Food & Pharmacy, a grocery retail chain based in the Pacific Northwest. Haggen went through tremendous growth through acquisitions in 2016, which actually seems to have hindered their company and set them back. Random fact for you: in 1989, Haggen was the first grocery store to include an in-store Starbucks, probably before most of you had even heard of Starbucks. The company was founded in 1933, and by 2014 they were had 18 stores with 16 pharmacies, which is a great family run business success. Then they got the acquisition bug, and in 2014 went from 18 to 164 stores, and 16 to 106 pharmacies. They went from 2,000 employees to 10,000 employees almost overnight. By September 2015, they had filed for bankruptcy. The full scope and history of Haggen is not done justice by just one paragraph, but the point is, acquiring for growth is a great way to increase top line, but you have to be concerned and focused on the integration. For those interested in this case study, I recommend reading more about the history and the pros and cons of their strategies, as well as the debates about what they did right and what they did wrong. A simple internet search will yield extensive results on this topic.

Fact: You can't take your eye off the ball.

You expect a certain quality. Hopefully your new company and employees have the same expectation. Your partners and managers have their work cut out for them, as all it takes is one employee who is lazy or untrained to create issues. One of the companies I worked with had a little more than $5 million in revenue, but it was a $50,000 project that caused their downfall. The small project turned out to have issues, and a subsequent lawsuit, bad press, and settlement out of court destroyed the culture and made it impossible for the company to continue in their market. They were eventually broken up into separate entities.

<u>Steps for integration that you should address.</u>

You should have a detailed integration action plan broken out by key areas. Create your own checklist based on all of the deliverables and action items you want to put in place. If you search the internet for 'merger integration action plan by department' and click on 'images,' you will find a plethora of examples. Some of the areas to be addressed will be Accounting, Human Resources, Legal, Insurance, Information Technology, Marketing, Operations, Sales and Intellectual Property (if any).

Here are examples, but definitely not an all-inclusive list from some of the areas:

Management Team / Advisers Actions

- these will constitute everything from organization structure / charts to strategic plans, executive scorecards, notifications to suppliers / customers / suppliers, marketing plan, sales plan, picking a law firm / accounting firm and other professional services can be consolidated to one company, and finalizing the budget for the combined entity.
- additional action steps will depend on how detailed your board is, if you have an advisory board (which you should), and if you want to add someone from the industry to your board of directors, approving the combined budgets for the coming year and the updated business plan, 30/60/90 day targets, one page strategic plan, and restating your vision.

Marketing Team Actions

- some items to be hammered out include web / social media strategy, brochures, signage, web, ads, other collateral material, integration of company messaging and positioning with the buyer's staff, and company proposal updates.

Sales Team Actions

- these include cross selling opportunities, CRM training, new vendor initiatives, sales quotas, comparison of salary / bonus plans, case studies of joint customers (this will help in future acquisitions as well as with customers / vendors), best practice sharing and sales organization chart.

Accounting Actions

- VERY important to get these teams coordinated.
- financial plan for the next 12 - 24 months, integration of accounting processes, supplier and vendor negotiations, insurance review, purchasing authorization levels, contracts and credit approval processes.

Human Resources Actions

- contractor and employee non-disclosure agreements, full 'on boarding' of new hires, policies and procedures, employee handbook, employee score cards into file, review of 401k program, and compensation review.

Operations to do's

- supplier and vendor review, product ordering processes, contract review process, review with legal team all corporate documents and processes.

Other Administrative Actions

- IT security review of ALL new computers accessing the network, confirming software licenses on all systems, ERP strategy, vendor discounts based on increased spend, company automobile and telephone policies, identification and recording of company assets.

The above are just a small sample of action items.

The action plan should be organized by department and include, at a minimum (1) primary owner, (2) target completion date, (3) actual completion date, and (4) comments to add in specific deliverables. On larger action items (such as selecting and ERP system, vendor reviews, marketing strategies) you will likely have a secondary support owner.

The completion, or at least onset, of this process can begin prior to signing the documents. You, your business partners and the owner(s) of the acquisition will likely already know who you want to lead the charge on specific items, even if those people do not yet know about the transaction. While this may seem like a lot, it will take much less time to discuss these items with your team now rather than waiting until something goes wrong and people are looking around saying, "Why didn't we think of that?"

Depending on the size of your company and your acquisition, you should strongly consider hiring an outside strategy consultant to help plan the transition. Yes, you probably 'could' do it yourself, but you cannot facilitate and participate in the process at the same time. This will be money very well spent.

Cash management

The overall objective of cash management is to learn to identify areas of your business that you could enhance for positive improvements. The concepts are simple at the outset, and the benefits are exponential if you are able to properly apply them to your business. The same concept applies to your acquisitions. If you are buying a business valued at $10 million and you do nothing to improve it, then you have done yourself (and the business) no benefits. You need to focus on what levers you can pull to have a chain reaction for improvements. Those levers you pull will be in all aspects from payment terms, to vendor terms, A/R, merchant fees, and bank payments. The improvement does not have to be earth shattering, but you should be focused every day on improving these areas so that overall growth can occur.

Customer integration

We discussed in an earlier chapter the importance of increasing the value to the customer to increase the value of the customer. This can be done by increasing the number of transactions per year or lengthening the duration of the relationship. Remember, customers of the company you just acquired will be on high alert. Stories circulate about how a vendor is acquired and customer service goes down. You have to go above and beyond to keep them happy. They might be waiting, anticipating that you will screw up. Not because they have bad intentions, just bad prior experiences. Take advantage of your opportunities to prove them wrong.

This might mean taking the customer to lunch even if you do not like going to client lunches. Some companies don't feel they have time to go for vendor lunches. They just want to see that service does not slack off. More specifically, they do not want to deal with the headache of their employees complaining about you. I do <u>not</u> suggest a luncheon at your office where you invite the customers to come to you to hear about how the acquisition is a good deal. Unless you have a really cool warehouse or company tour that people want to see, go to the customer or just call them. Keeping them as a customer is much easier than trying to find a replacement customer for when that one leaves because you didn't give them attention.

This is how you solidify your brand, which is a new brand for them. Your 'new' customer will decide about your based on what they hear from their employees. The last thing you want them to hear are comments that your company is "not as good as it was when Brent was the owner."

With all the work you have put in to obtaining customers, now is the time to make sure they are happy so you retain them.

CHAPTER 17

Duplicative Costs/Surviving Culture

There are many reasons that an acquisition is a good idea. We have covered them throughout this book.

1. Growth - there are many definitions of this. There is growth in revenue, growth in locations, grown in assets under management, or even growth in number of staff.
2. Money - this is a great strategy if you are looking to create a job for yourself or to create an investment, to generate higher cash flow for your business.
3. Ego - if you are doing it for this purpose, stop. Pride comes before the fall. There is no reason to proceed further. You are messing around with peoples' jobs and it's not worth it.

Is 1 + 1 > 2 for the deal to work?

I am sure there are countless other reasons, but the reason to do the acquisition is 1 + 1 has to equal more than 2. What I mean is this acquisition will lead you to a new market or a new city or diversity your customer base so you have less of a concentration risk or you will move yourself up higher on the valuation chart.

As discussed earlier, simply doing the acquisition to make yourself more valuable can be a good idea. Just be cognizant of any increased risks you inherit. Growth for the sake of growth is not always a great idea. However, if you are planning on selling your entire organization in a handful of years, then the growth may just be the piece of the puzzle you are looking for.

With larger acquisitions, when it's time to sell, there will be a quality of earnings audit done, which basically looks to see what non-recurring expenses can be removed, owner costs added back, etc. This way the true value of the acquisition will be discovered.

It is important to remember your margin of error.

In statistics, margin of error will tell you the range. So if 54% of people support a specific initiative in an upcoming vote, but there is a margin of error of 5%, that means you should expect the final result to be somewhere in the 49% - 59% range of what the final vote will be.

In acquiring a business, the same is true. If based on projections and due diligence you are expecting to earn $150,000 in earnings from an acquisition, at the end of the year, if you earn $135,000 or $165,000, you shouldn't be too surprised.

Saving $ and getting rid of duplicative costs

One of the quickest ways to monetize the transaction is to eliminate duplicative costs.

Duplicative costs are costs that you and the selling business both currently pay and that after the acquisition, you should not both be paying. Imagine that before your wedding, you and your fiancé both have newspaper subscriptions, cable, and utilities. You get married and move in together, and now you have no need for two newspaper subscriptions, two cable services and two water bills. Yes, I know the example is from long ago when everyone had a print newspaper subscription, but just trying to make the point.

The most obvious duplicative cost in an acquisition is rent. There are a couple of components here, as the seller might very well have a lease that has anywhere from six months to two+ years left on it (unless the timing is perfect). Some other obvious factors are, (1) do you need both locations, (2) do you have the space to house everyone, (3) depending on the type of business, is their location important for your client base, (4) can you keep the address but down size or partition the space as you are moving some functions out and lower the cost, and (5) is their space or location better than yours?

In terms of the location being important for their (and your) client base, some of this depends on the industry. If your industry is one where customers will not travel more than 5 - 10 miles from their home for your service, then, yes, it is important. In 2014, BrightLocal.com completed a survey to find out how far people would travel in 13 different industries. Gym came in at 12 minutes, while Doctor came in around 22 minutes. Restaurants, realtor, accountant, hairdresser came in-between the 12 – 22 minute range. What wasn't asked was, would you travel 15 minutes for something that used to be 5 minutes away? That is the key. People are creatures of habit, if your following is strong enough, they will follow if you move. Ask them and see what they say.

We acquired a CPA firm on the other side of town (about 30 - 45 minutes travel time depending on traffic). I had no intent or desire to ever go to that office, but it turned out to be a great location for our existing customers on that side of town to drop off their work. So just because YOU do not want to go to that office, there may still be a good business reason for keeping it. In this case we had customers driving 30 minutes who now only needed to drive 10 minutes, so they loved it.

Buying a business is not the same thing as opening a second location. There can be similarities, but there are definite additional things you need to consider before starting a second location.

In terms of this chapter, rent is a duplicative cost, as once the acquisition is done, you will be able to transfer their employees and customers to your location.

The same is true for utilities, security system, internet, water, janitorial, and other office and/or warehouse overhead.

Other potential items to factor in to your projections:

- Property and casualty insurance
- Errors and Omissions insurance
- Accounting fees
- Tax return prep fees
- Board of director or adviser fees
- Banking fees
- Web hosting fees and subscriptions
- Shipping fees (1)
- Payroll service fees (2)
- Marketing fees (3)
- Other professional fees, such as outsourced IT services, strategy consultants

(1) Yes, you will still be shipping a lot, but this is where your increased volume will kick in to help. For one of our acquisitions, we contacted both UPS and FedEx and told them, "We are combining the purchasing power of both entities and would like a discount." The new company was able to negotiate a discount which equated to an approximately $80,000 per year savings from what the two companies were paying separately.

(2) Depending on your size, most companies should consider a Professional Employment Organization (PEO), which, aside from reducing risk and offering more benefits, will help the on-boarding process for your new employees go much smoother. Even if you do not go the PEO route, you should have reduced payroll processing fees regardless of who you use.

(3) You may not want to reduce your marketing fees, but if you both have a marketing agency of record, you can consolidate down to one agency to control the message.

Some of the above will be eliminated; all should at a minimum be reduced.

It is very important to recognize that you may not have the best / most efficient / most economical option, so it might be that it is some of your vendors, not just theirs, that will be cut in the process.

Surviving Culture

It has been my experience that the company doing the buying for the most part has the surviving culture. When that has not been the case, it has been because the company which is being bought has more people, more efficiencies, and/or more footprint in the field, etc. One of the classic case studies in this regard is when Amazon.com bought Zappos for about $837 million in 2009. Zappos was adamant that they (Zappos) would 'retain their independent culture and its way of doing business.' There are very few Amazons and very few Zappos in terms of what we are talking about here, but do not make a snap judgment about which one will survive. Make it a priority to communicate on this early on, before you sign on the dotted line. Make sure the culture king or culture queen of each company gets to meet. These are the people who know what it will take to make it work. Use the opportunity to foster growth for both cultures (remember you are not just doing the transaction to increase revenue!).

I have seen some cultural differences between office locations, but the overall culture and core values of the organization should be the same. The Vision of the company that you and your team have should be shared with all employees at the very first meeting. If you have a Painted Picture or other visual display about what you want the organization to look and feel like, then that needs to be presented on Day 1. Frankly, before you ever get to Day 1, at t-minus 60 days and counting, before you get to term sheets with potential acquisitions, you should find out about their culture, explain your culture, and discuss how your vision, core values, and your top people function.

Just as you have a sales team meeting to plan, or a combined marketing team meeting to plan, you also have a culture team meet to plan. This is important. These are the people that 90% of your employees will look to, to see if they think it was a good transaction. Just as business owners are people, so are employees. Employees have questions and fears, think them through. If you skip this step it will take longer and require more effort in the future.

Doing an acquisition that brings on people who do not fit your core values or culture will just disrupt everything you have spent so much time building.

On several occasions, the culture of the acquired company did not mesh with the buying company, and while they both continued to hit their numbers, we never saw a good integration. Even at annual Christmas parties or company events, you could feel the tension of an "Our office vs Their office" mentality. For what it is worth, in the long run, neither of these two acquisitions end up working themselves out as there were internal conflicts (not huge), but it was never a "we" it was always "Us vs. Them". Just because they are in the same industry does not mean they think / act / feel / believe / dream / have vision the same way as your team.

It may have taken a while for your most loyal employees to embrace your business and brand, so do not expect the new employees to do this any faster.

In 2008, Sprint announced it was writing down 80% of the value of Nextel, a company it had acquired in 2005 for $35 billion. Many believe the acquisition was doomed from the start, with Nextel being 'more khaki culture' and Sprint being 'buttoned down formal with bureaucratic management.' By 2012 they had gotten rid of Nextel completely, and *CNET* called it "a concluding chapter in one of the worst mergers in history."

Key point: on the subjects of both duplicative costs and surviving culture. It is important to remember to keep an open mind about the process. King Solomon, long revered as the wisest person to ever live, said, "When pride comes, then comes disgrace, but with the humble is wisdom." (Proverbs 11:2, ESV) Do not presume your way is the best way. In fact, in many ways you should be pleasantly surprised if the vendors or the culture of the company you are acquiring are better, as that is just another intangible benefit you have received!

CHAPTER 18

What If It Does Not Work Out?

While we earlier focused on answers to challenges you might encounter during the transaction, this chapter is focused on challenges you could run into after the transaction.

The Exit Planning Institute calls the process for a business owner deciding to sell, the three legs of the stool. The three legs are: (1) 'Personal Financial Planning,' basically, being financially ready; (2) 'maximizing of business value,' or business valued as much as possible; (3) 'Life After Business Planning' or the business owner being ready to retire.

Sometimes you will do a transaction based on the seller's representations of the business. Sometimes the seller will have misrepresented on purpose, sometimes by accident, and sometimes things just happen.

During the first phase of the process you need to determine if you want the seller remaining part of the business. I have had nightmare scenarios with the seller remaining on and wanting to meddle with everything we were doing, to the point of us having to ask them to resign as they were hindering the growth. Another seller made more with us than she was being offered by other people, but still complained as she did not like the way things played out for her personally. I have also had scenarios where the selling shareholder moves into sales and excels beyond what we both had imagined. There is no shortage of scenarios where everyone wins.

However, there will always be the chance someone will not be happy, even if you deliver on everything you said. Just fair warning.

Sometimes, you do not want the seller to stay on, but they say it is a requirement of the deal for them to stay on for a certain period of time. That is honestly a tough call. It depends on their personality and if they adhere to your company core values. If they do not, then I would say it is a deal breaker. Sometimes they do adhere to the core values as an owner, but once they become your employee, it is like Dr. Jekyll and Mr. Hyde and they go off the rails. This is not a situation you want to get yourself into, so if the seller would like to continue working, you should take the steps necessary to analyze if they will fit into your culture AND, most importantly, if they can relinquish control and decision making to you. If they are still around, their employees will likely look to them for their buy in, or even let them in on company secrets (not intentionally), just because they always have done so.

I know an entrepreneur who will not consider any acquisition in which the selling shareholders stay employed. He says in his experience it has always caused culture issues and it just creates conversations that you do not want to have.

From experience, much of this can be determined from personality studies or tendency analysis of the selling shareholders (and whoever will be their supervisor). The most effective ones I have used are The Predictive Index (PI), www.predictiveindex.com, and Myers Briggs, www.myersbriggs.org. We did those on a selling shareholder, along with our CEO and CFO, and found the selling shareholder was a narcissist and would never work well with the CEO and CFO. He was great to talk with, plan, talk strategize, etc., but when it came to them being on the job together, the adviser we hired to coach us in the process said trying to get everyone working together was a waste of time. The surveys cost less than $100 each, but saved us countless hours by identifying and addressing issues early on in the process.

What happens when it does not work out?

This is a reality you have to be prepared for. You need to address this when preparing the documents and discuss it with the seller.

The seller will likely push for a transaction in which you carry 100% of the risk. You are buying the business, you issue a promissory note, and you make payments. Often this will be what they are looking for.

However, if you are doing a merger or some other form of joint venture, or there is a seller carried note, there may be a provision the seller (or you) wants to have that if you do not make payments, they have the right to take back the business.

The transaction not working out could come in many forms.

Maybe you want to sell the larger company down the road and they do not want to, so they build the ability to object or call their note due into the agreements if you sell within a certain period.

Maybe you do not get along. Irreconcilable differences can happen between business partners, too.

Maybe their customer base did not come over as seamlessly as expected.

Maybe you just do not feel they are living up to their end of the bargain!

There are many reasons why it may not work out. It is best for you to discuss what happens if it does not work out BEFORE you complete the acquisition.

Does everyone just take their toys home with them? Once the company is integrated (especially with branding), that will be hard to do. You should have something in the agreement about what you pay to them for their customers who choose to stay with you. What would you pay a normal referral fee? That should be fair. However, you need to be prepared to receive only the same amount if the customers leave to go back to them.

You should discuss and document all the scenarios you can come up with to make sure you both agree on what the plan will be. Most attorneys will recommend a buy-sell agreement, or at least including language in your agreements to cover what happens if you can't come to an agreement on how to move forward. In this day and age this is more and more common place.

Sometimes it is as clear as, "If we do not agree and cannot come to an agreement, we will have a third party chosen by our CPA to do an independent appraisal. At that time, Partner 1 will have the ability to buy out Partner 2 for the respective value. The terms of that buyout will be monthly payments over 36 months."

Sometimes it is more complex, with steps both parties have to take to try and resolve the disagreement, inclusive of:

- Hiring third party business coach (I have seen one hire a therapist for the business owners)
- Appointing unrelated third party as swing vote
- Hiring 3 appraisers and averaging the appraisals
- Skip the appraisal and have Partner 1 make offer to Partner 2. If Partner 2 accepts, Partner 1 pays it, if Partner 2 rejects it, then Partner 2 has to buy out Partner 1
- List for sale

How detailed or complex you want this to get is up to you, based on your own comfort level. But regardless, this pre-nuptial, or divorce clause, as many refer to it, is critical in saving you headaches down the road should the merger not play out the way you both expect.

Some of them are too integrated to be split up

If your integration team does their job well, it will be very hard to split up the two companies. The split could get messy, and it is best for both parties to line out their expectations of what will happen should this occur.

We had an acquisition of a CPA firm that, for many reasons, did not work out. We did some things wrong, they did some things wrong, and then some things just did not go as either of us would have wanted. Because we had acquired them, we let them go back to running their own practice. They slowly changed their name and moved into a new location. That was four years ago. The reason this split went so smoothly is we both made sure this was an easy split for the employees and the customers.

One of the key points is something we discussed earlier. Business owners are people too. They have families, friends, children, spouses. If things do not work out, be as civil as you can and be cognizant of the fact that the transaction was a leap of faith on both parts, so unwinding it will not be pleasurable to either party. On one merger that did not work out, one of parties took the breakup hard, and we ended up having to hire an attorney to pursue the money owed to us. It was not a fun process, and after all was said and done, the money that we 'won' almost all went to the attorneys. Winning out of principal is the only result sometimes, and it is a long road to get there.

CHAPTER 19

Summary, Next Steps and What You Can Do Now

We are at the end of the road. Writing this book has been a great experience for me, as well as putting on to paper my years of experience, good and bad, being a party to many different deals.

I cannot promise you will acquire $100 million in revenue (I am not sure I would even recommend it!), but what I can promise you, is that if you follow these steps, you will have an almost endless supply of potential acquisitions. How you structure those acquisitions / mergers / transactions will be up to you, and I just hope I have shared enough experience with you to give you some suggested paths to go down.

During all the different phases of acquisition in all the companies I have worked with, I have usually had a partner in the process with whom I would share ideas and goals about what the acquisitions would look like and how we would find them. This is important. You cannot underestimate the value of having a second set of eyes / brain / person to talk through the deal points. You can certainly do this on your own, but having a partner will definitely make it easier.

Doing an acquisition is like hosting a Thanksgiving feast. Timing becomes important, as there are many moving pieces (kids getting hungry, do not want to overcook the turkey, other hot dishes getting cold). Making sure everyone has something they want and, ideally, that everyone leaves the meal feeling great. Is it possible to do it all on your own? Sure. However, would your stress level be lower if you had help? Certainly.

Once we started the process as laid out in this book, we found we were inundated with potential acquisitions.

Prepare yourself! You do not want to be the dog chasing the car who catches it but doesn't know what to do. You need to prepare for the next steps of what happens after the acquisition. I can promise you, the act of finding, negotiating, and acquiring the business was <u>not</u> the hardest part; the integration after the acquisitions was where the real work came to be needed. This is where you need to make sure you have a great team ready for the challenge. They might do a great job when you on-board one or two employees at a time, but what about 10 new employees, or even 50 new employees? How about 50 employees and 300 new customers? Now you will find out what they can really handle.

- The most interesting part of this is how things can change in an instant. What if right now you are thinking you want do to four acquisitions, each in the $2 million - $5 million range? Now fast forward; the first one is done and you are ready to start on the second one. From there, your perspective will likely change.

1st Acquisition: So if you start out as a $4 million dollar business looking to buy a $2 million dollar business. That is 50% of your size.

2nd Acquisition: After that is done you are now a $6 million dollar business looking to buy a $2 million dollar business. That is 33% of your size.

3rd Acquisition: After that one, you are now an $8 million dollar business looking to buy a $2 million dollar business. That is 25% of your size.

4th Acquisition: Now you are a $10 million dollar business looking to buy a $2 million dollar business. That is 20% of your size.

The entire landscape and make up of your company will change from the first to the fourth acquisition, so just be sure to reevaluate your position along the way and see what you need to hit your target and goals. You will more than likely say to yourself one of the following:

- Keep buying according to the plan
- Buy few businesses, but those with more revenue
- Don't buy anymore, just focus on digesting what we have bought

From experience, there is strength in each one of those positions. It depends where you, your company, your partners, your employees, the market, and a dozen other factors are at that time. You may have an appetite for more acquisitions, but the rest of the company may still be dealing with aftermath of the last one and not ready to digest another.

It is important to be aware of how everyone is doing throughout the process. You might have planned this whole endeavor because your accounting department was working at about 50% capacity. They work great at that volume, but now that you have them at 85% capacity, make sure the wheels aren't falling off.

Continue to evaluate the people you have in the organization. One of my best friends, who runs a large company here in Las Vegas, shared something with me about 10 years ago that I keep in mind to this day. I have shared it already, but it is worth repeating. One of his mentors took him and his partner to lunch and said, "The people you see here at $10 million in revenue won't be the same people you have at $30 million in revenue and they won't be the same people at $50 million in revenue." The point is, as you grow, you need to pause and make sure you have right people to get you through the next leg of the journey. You also need to make sure all the people have the same vision.

Another way of looking at this is, the people who got you from point A to point B, may not be the people the company needs when you go from point B to point C.

Most importantly… this includes YOU.

You need to be prepared and humble enough that when the company gets to a certain level, you might need to step aside and take on a different role. You may be the right person to lead the company now, but just make sure you are humble enough to see your own blind spots and have people around you who will tell you when you need to step aside.

You should also be prepared, and prepare your business, that while you are capitalizing on an age shift in the market, you do not miss how it could affect your own business in a few years. The U.S. Bureau of Labor Statistics, Current Population Survey lists the following industries as employing over than 60% of their workers over the age of 45.

	% of workers age 45+
Postal Service	72.0
Other general government and support	70.7
Funeral homes, and cemeteries and crematories	66.1
Bus service and urban transit	66.1
Personal and household goods repair and maintenance	64.9
Labor unions	64.0
Religious organizations	63.9
Sewage treatment facilities	63.6
Sewing, needlework, and piece goods stores	63.2
Electric and gas, and other combinations	62.7
Carpet and rug mills	62.0
Administration of economic programs and space research (Public administration)	61.9
Offices of other health practitioners	61.5
Textile product mills, except carpet and rug	61.3
Public finance activities	61.1
Fuel dealers	60.5
Libraries and archives	60.5

Aircraft and parts manufacturing	60.5
Water, steam, air-conditioning, and irrigation systems	60.3
Wholesale electronic markets, agents and brokers	60.0

If you are in one of those industries, there are great opportunities for those companies that are prepared. On the other hand, there are great challenges for those who sit on the sidelines waiting for someone else to let them know how to respond.

Make sure you are not so focused on opportunities 'out there' that you ignore those in your own backyard.

In summary, here is your checklist, or quick reference guide, of how you can grow your business by Identifying, Acquiring, and Repeating your process:

Summary of Steps

Step 1:   Find the industry you want to go after (you may already be in that industry), move to Step 2

Step 2:   Find industry research on the owners of these businesses, move to Step 3

Step 3:   Determine what you bring to the table, why would someone sell to you, move to Step 4

Step 4:   Make it known to the market that you are looking to buy, move to Step 5

Step 5:   Contact potential sellers, move to Step 6

Step 6:   Due diligence, move to Step 7

Step 7:   Structure the deal with everyone's best interest in mind, move to Step 8

Step 8:   Plan the integration, move to Step 9

Step 9:   Transition team, notification to all stakeholders, move to Step 10

Step 10: Monetize the transaction for everyone, move to Step 11

Step 11: Repeat Step 5 (every now and then you have to do Step 4 again)

So what you can do now?

If you are in an industry with companies you want to acquire, come up with a list of competitors and just call, email, or write them and say you are interested in expanding, and ask them if they would be interested in selling or merging.

If you do not have a business or industry in mind, start doing the research. Determine if you want to acquire a business to actively work in, or if you want to be a passive investor.

Do your research.

If you look up the highest profit margin industries, or look for industries with disproportionate amount of aging owners, maybe that is your start?

Maybe you are friends with a large vendor. If so take them to lunch and ask them who their buyers are, and if there is any benefit in you contacting the buyers about a roll up strategy to consolidate the administrative side.

There are many service firms that have high profit margins that this may fit into for you. However, the licensing process may be a hurdle you don't want to or can't get over. Is it a trade that requires licensing, is that going to slow you down?

This is a journey. Once you start down this path you will learn a lot about your business, yourself and the entire process. It is not always easy, but it is definitely rewarding. I was working with a company on a deal that took four months to get done, but in the end they acquired a company with $1.3 million in annual revenue. When the deal was done, the owner said to me, "I should just focus on doing these!" We discussed how long it would have taken him to acquire $100,000 a month in new revenue, and he said, "Much longer than what this took!"

On one of my early business card layouts had the following quote (of mine) and I feel it is appropriate here.

"The one who takes the first step is much farther than the one still thinking about what their first step will be."

I wish you the best in your endeavors. If I can ever be of assistance, please feel free to contact me. To learn more, please visit www.YesIf.com or follow me on Twitter @jasonfgriffith

RESOURCES AND SUGGESTED READINGS

This is not your typical "resources" page.

The following are books and movies which I recommend you read / listen to / watch to get a general understanding of what you are getting yourself into with acquisitions.

The movies are mostly for entertainment purposes, with brief points that can be applied to your situation.

<u>Books:</u>

Thinking Fast and Slow (Kahneman)
Game Changer (McAdams)
The Checklist Manifesto (Gawande)
Profit First (Michalowicz)
The One Thing (Keller / Papasan)
Peak (Ericsson, Pool)
Breakthrough Company (McFarland)
Lateral Thinking (De Bono)
The Art of Storytelling (Walsh)
Traction / Get a Grip (Paton / Wickman)
Scaling Up (Harnish)
David and Goliath (Gladwell)
Make Big Happen (Moses)
Double Double (Herold)
Cracking the Code (Bly)
Nudge (Thaler)

The Black Swan: Impact of Highly Improbable (Taleb)
The E-Myth (Gerber)
The Science of Getting Rich (Wattles)
Paper Napkin Wisdom (Jayaraman/Daly)
Grinding it Out: The Making of McDonald's (Kroc)
Built to Sell (Warrillow)

Movies:

Secret of My Success
Other People's Money
The Game
The Hudsucker Proxy

EXHIBITS

The exhibits on the following pages are just examples that you can use, adjust, alter or completely ignore. I am not an attorney, nor am I offering tax or legal advice in the documents or in this book, I encourage you to seek your own counsel for both of these matters prior to entering into any transaction. The documents are meant to be a guide and to stimulate some ideas and internal discussions as you prepare for your acquisitions and plan for the execution of the specific items.

For electronic versions of these to download for Free please visit www.YesIf.com or follow me on Twitter @jasonfgriffith

Exhibit List

1. Client Communication Handout
2. Employee announcement letter / email
3. Welcome letter to new POD
4. Company Acquisition Program FAQ to go over with potential sellers
5. Acquisition FAQ – for selling owner
6. POD FAQ for Daily Operations
7. FAQ on POD for employees and sellers

8. FAQ: HR, Payroll and Benefits – for employees
9. Merger / Acquisition – What does this mean for me (for employees)
10. Transition Team Ideas
11. Example acquisition strategy time line
12. Example letter of intent
13. Example POD Agreement

Client Communication Handout - this is what we give to all new employees.

Communication is the #1 complaint I hear when talking with someone about why they don't like their vendor (whether us or competitor).

Put yourself in the client's shoes, you are paying thousands of dollars for a task. Email and phone are the primary means of communication, with email being the preferred choice the majority of the time.

The amount of feedback / follow-up received from you increases the perceived value in the client's mind.

Clients do not complain about service or bills, if they can "see" the value. Even if there is no update to give, check in with them by forwarding the last update and say "John, Just wanted to check back with you and let you know we are still waiting on the documents below from your attorney / agent / bank (or whoever). Please let me know if we can help in the meantime, thanks."

Occasionally you may forget; however, respond as soon as you remember. By not responding at all, the client begins to question their choice to engage us, they wonder if we are really working on their project and eventually worry if they will finish on time.

So, it is important that when they check their email, they see / hear from you: the more the better. It makes you look bad to say you will respond and then you don't respond.

When to respond?

Minimum within 8-hours. Even if the response is to just acknowledge receipt. "John, I wanted to confirm receipt of your email, I will try and get back to you by _____, at the latest". This lets the client know you received their request and you will be in touch soon. Again, chances are, if you fail to respond it may lead them to believe you are ignoring them. Years ago 24 hours used to be good enough response, then 8 hours, but now there are many companies who require their employees to respond much sooner than that. I know of one which says if they are in the office they have to respond within 30 minutes, even if it is to just acknowledge receipt and tell the customer you are looking into it.

I imagine each of you goes through your own to do list to see what you are waiting on from clients, so why not email them at the same time? All you need to do is take the last email you sent them, delete the stuff you already have, and send it again.

How often to follow-up?

If you are waiting on information, you should be emailing them AT LEAST once every week to follow up. Put a note in Outlook if you need to, or just make every Friday at 4 pm, the time you email every client you are working on to provide them a status. I have NEVER heard a company or person say "Damn, my accountant follows up with me way too much!" This will prevent clients from following up with us. One of the top pet peeves of the partners is when clients follow up with us. Chances are clients / people, realize they don't know what's going on with their project long before they actually take the step to send an email (while cc'ing everyone else in the process).

What to say?

- 95% of all responses start with or contain "Thank you" in the first sentence or two. Thank you for the email, the questions, the information, etc.

- 95% of all emails end with a version of the phrase "Please let me know if you have any questions." Or something similar to let the client know if we haven't answered all of their questions to let us know.
- Don't make responding to their emails seem like a burden.
- All initial emails should be signed with your name and the company details. Don't send emails that aren't signed.

Sometimes internally there are many emails on the same subject back and forth where it's obviously ok, but to clients you should sign the email.

Sending multiple emails / replies back and forth to client do not need full email signature, but at least use your first name.

- Read the whole email, nothing is worse than if you respond to an email with a question and they have already answered the question in the email. It shows a lack of respect for the time of the person who sent it to you;
- Make sure you answer all the questions; Figure out the point of the email, they may ask a bunch of questions, but the point of the email is "when are we going to file" or "have you heard back from the investors" – and make sure that is addressed too;
- If you don't feel comfortable with the response, draft one and ask your manager or partner for their review;
- When asking for assistance, provide a suggestion or solution. Do NOT forward the email to a partner or manager and ask "how should I respond". This is a great way to learn; and most important,
- Sometimes an email is not appropriate, you need to call. If the client is angry or upset, that may be one of those times, but documenting the call via email (after the call) helps make sure expectations are on the same page too.
- When you send changes to the client, let the client know what you expect them to do and what they can expect after.
- Same with the format of documents. If you want a spreadsheet reconciliation then say that otherwise they may just send you something via email that you have to re-type / enter to calculate

Client Communication

- If the topic of an email is complicated, send an example template if the email sounds like they are confused. It may help them understand.
- Most (if not all) people you communicate with can't read your mind. You need to be clear and say what you information you are looking for / need. Don't assume they know what you are talking about. If you don't ask for it in the email, chances are you aren't going to get it
- Read the email aloud to yourself, this will catch most grammatical errors and spelling errors where the words are spelled right, but the wrong word (there vs their; our vs are).
- Ask yourself, would you say this to them on the phone / on a call? Emails can come across rude, remember you don't know the setting they are reading the email in.

Tools: Insert commonly used text.

- You can create a shortcut to add commonly used phrases, like "Please let me know if you have any questions."

Consider doing this process for other phrases that you type a lot.

- o Go to Tools and select AutoCorrect Options
- o In the *Replace Box*, type "plm"
- o In the *With* box, type "Please let me know if you have any questions."
- o Click Add.

Tools: Follow-up Reminders

- In Outlook
- o Tasks
- o Calendar
- o Flags and Reminders on emails

- To set a reminder on a new email message
o Click on the red flag reminder button:
o This will pop up a window so you can set a reminder to Follow Up (as you just promised):
o The two "None" fields above are where you select the date (on left) and time (on right) for the follow up reminder.

We are here to provide you with the tools to get the job done. If you need something, you need to say what tools you need to succeed at your job. If you don't ask then we can't help you. Additionally, your managers and admin team are also here to assist. If you need something, you need to say something. If you do not ask for the tools to help you succeed, then shame on you. You need to say what tools you need to succeed at your job. Remember every email to the client is a communication which represents you, your colleagues, the partners, and the company, so don't embarrass yourself or us. ☺

I can promise you these suggestions will go leaps and bounds towards improving efficiency, client satisfaction and responsiveness.

NIGHTSTAND COMPANY LOGO

Team NIGHTSTAND,

As part of our continued growth strategy, NIGHTSTAND, Inc. today is announcing we are now part of SHADOW SERVICES, a regional food service company. We are a subsidiary of this company with a goal of continuing with their restaurant acquisition strategy. The majority of you should notice very little changes inside the company. Tyler will still be working with Steven Franklin and Brent Farnham at managing the company and we will be executing the same plans we have had since our founding, delivering quality meals with our first class team of chefs.

We are on track with growing locations and revenues as well as entertaining strategic acquisitions which could increase our offerings to customers. We have had a fantastic year last year and are positioned for more positive growth and performance. We thank you all for your work and encourage you to continue to perform at the top of this amazing city.

If you have any questions along the way, please feel free to reach out to me at any point in time.

Best regards,
NIGHTSTAND, Inc.

Tyler Vincent
President

January 18, 2017

Aaron Vision
WRIGLEY CORP, LLC
Address
City, State Zip

Dear Aaron,

Welcome to the **WRIGLEY CORP** family. We are very excited that you have made the decision to become part of our team, and participate in the building of the **WRIGLEY CORP** brand.

Over the next couple of weeks we will be forming the new operating LLC and handling all of the legal and administrative aspects associated therewith, including obtaining a business checking account. Each month a debit will come out of the checking account in the amount of 15% of the Gross Deposits that month for our Management Fee. We will monitor for items such as returned checks or capital contributions to insure the 15% is only paid on Client Deposits.

As well, we will begin setting up **Software 1, Software 2, and Software 3**, as well as transition you to our **CRM**. I understand that all of this takes time, and there are unique issues associated therewith, so please be patient throughout the process. Some initiatives are more urgent than others and we are sensitive to that, as well. We will transition the **Payroll Processing** function to **WRIGLEY CORP** in accordance with your schedule, but please remember that effective today your Payroll is chargeable to the new entity.

We encourage you to get to know our staff and get a feel for our culture at **WRIGLEY CORP** so feel free to stop by our offices at your convenience. If you know of any other companies which may be interested in joining **WRIGLEY CORP** please let me know and I will personally reach out to them. A reminder that you will receive a $10,000 Fee for any companies you refer to us which become part of **WRIGLEY CORP.**

On behalf of **WRIGLEY CORP**, thank you very much for becoming part of our company, and we are excited about the opportunity to grow your company along with you.

Warm Regards,

Collin Franklin
President

WRIGLEY CORP, LLC
Las Vegas, Nevada
Your Company Acquisition Checklist

FAQ's: WRIGLEY CORP Firm Acquisition Program

Below please find some of the most common questions that prospective Partners ask about joining WRIGLEY CORP. To discuss your specific situation, please call _____.

How will merging into with WRIGLEY CORP benefit my Practice?

You will be joining a growing, established Firm that has a strong reputation in the community. Your practice will be able to operate under a known brand, and you will be able to reduce costs, work as much or little as you want, and have a built in exit strategy.

Can I continue working for as long as I want?

Yes, if you do not want to retire yet, you may continue servicing your clientele for as long as you desire.

At what price and under what terms will WRIGLEY CORP buy my practice?

We will buy your Practice at a factor of 0.90 of Gross Revenues as determined over a three period by of collections and paid over that time. After you have been with WRIGLEY CORP for five years, we reserve the right to purchase your Practice from you at that price.

Will I continue working in the same office and under the same structure?

Our goal is a smooth transition for you into WRIGLEY CORP. If staying in your current office makes sense for both of us, then that is fine with us. Your phone numbers will change to reflect your new association with our firm. The legal structure will be a new LLC where you and WRIGLEY CORP are both LLC Members.

Will I be able to trim down my professional and administrative employees?

Yes. WRIGLEY CORP has an internal structure of professional labor that will lower your overall costs precipitously. You will leverage our resources and network to lower your administrative and firm operating costs, as well.

What professional support with I get and how much will it cost?

We will provide a range of services to you, from new employee to experienced managers. We will charge you an amount which we will agree upon in advance given the project at hand. You will be able to accept projects which you would not otherwise accept (due to labor or time or knowledge constraints), and be able to benefit from those even if you do none of the actual work.

Who will be responsible for forming the new operating LLC?

We will begin by forming the new operating LLC.

Who will be responsible for setting up the bank account(s)?

We will coordinate the setting-up of the business checking account.

Who will coordinate the IT and software transition?

We will coordinate any IT and software needs. The software includes programs such as: _____, _____, and _____ (insert **industry software programs and others you use**). We will be handling the legal, administrative and technical aspects associated with these changes.

Who will be handling the transition of HR, payroll and benefits?

We will transition the Payroll Processing function to the current human resource, benefits and payroll services provider. Additional details will be provided detailing this changeover, payroll schedules and available benefits. Please remember, effective _____, payroll is chargeable to the new entity. You will likely have to do a 'final payroll' for the employees on your system before they come to ours.

How is the monthly Management Fee paid?

We will debit the checking account each month for the monthly Management Fee. The Management Fee will be ____% **(I have seen as low as 4% and as high as 15%)** of the Gross Deposits for that month. We will review activity for such items as returned checks and capital contributions to insure the ____% is paid only on Client Deposits and not on reimbursements or intercompany transfers. As a reminder, please provide a detailed list of your Fees for the last 12 months, at your earliest convenience, so we can work on the projections with you.

Do you offer a bonus for Company referrals to the WRIGLEY CORP Acquisition Program?

Yes, if you know of other Company's which may be interested in joining WRIGLEY CORP, please let us know. You will receive a $3,500 Bonus for any Company you refer that becomes a part of WRIGLEY CORP. **(I have seen this as flat amount and other's as a sliding scale)**

FAQ: Owner Contact Call List

IF YOU ARE SMALL ENOUGH, THE ANSWER TO ALL OF THESE MAY BE YOU, BUT IT IS SOMETHING YOU SHOULD HAVE

1. Who can answer my payroll questions?
2. Who can help with my company licensing?
3. Who is my Integration Team leader?
4. Who can help me with marketing questions?
5. Who can help me with company branding questions?
6. Who can help me with questions related to _____ services or _____ product ordering?
7. Who can help me with customer questions regarding products you offer that I have never offered?
8. Who can help me with customer payment options?
9. Who can assist me with quoting fees?
10. Who can assist me with billing questions?
11. Who is my IT contact?

FAQ Related to Daily Operations - WRIGLEY CORP 1 <POD Name>

Name changes

Q: When do we start answering the phone "WRIGLEY CORP"?

A: You should start answering the phone Wrigley Corp today.

Q: Will we be responsible for changing the name with vendors?

A: You will be provided with a standard letter to send out to all of you vendor making them aware of name change along with billing instructions.

Licenses

Q: We are unclear where we fall with the Company and where we have to have our own permits/licenses?

Q: Do we need a separate State of Nevada tax ID number for use tax and state unemployment? Do we fall under Corporate for unemployment?

Q: How about State Business tax?

Q: Our county Business license?

Q: Will the IRS have questions with the LLC tax id number for the new entity and the name being just Wrigley Corp?

A: Not likely. WRIGLEY CORP, LLC is the DBA for your POD.

Payroll

Q: When will the first pay period begin?

Q: Will the day we get paid change?

A: The pay dates will be the 8th and 23rd of each month. The pay periods are as follows 16th thru the EOM: paid on the 8th

1st thru the 15th: paid on the 23rd

The first payroll that will be processed through Payroll Co will be _____.

Additional details will be sent under separate cover.

Q: Will we see a change in our benefits? If so, when will these changes take place?

A: There will be no change at this time to the benefits currently being offered. However, a review of available plans will be conducted and new plans will be considered. Should it be determined that a change will be made, the proper notice will be provided.

Software

Q: Who will provide standardization of our software/systems?

A: All computer software will be standardized to Wrigley Corp's current software.

Q: Who is responsible for all updates and renewals?

A: All software updates will be handled through the Wrigley Corp main office.

Q: Do current licenses need to be changed to WRIGLEY CORP?

A: All software updates will be handled through the Wrigley Corp main office.

Benefits

Q: Will our company policies be changing?

A: Not at this time; however, the current employee handbook is being reviewed to ensure compliance with state and federal regulation. You will receive a copy of the handbook once finalized. We anticipate this will be complete by the middle of February.

Q: What will be the changes to our PTO/Vacation time?

A: There will be no change at this time to the benefits currently being offered, pending a review of the current employee handbook.

Q: Will we see a change in our benefits? If so, when will these changes take place?

A: There will be no change at this time to the benefits currently being offered. However, a review of available plans will be conducted and new plans will be considered. Should it be determined that a change will be made, the proper notice will be provided.

Other Miscellaneous:

Q: Will there be any advancement opportunities within the company?

A: Advancement opportunities will be considered based on employees' goals and the overall business needs of the organization.

Q: Where do I fit into the new organization?

A: Our Company has a culture of encouraging employees to set goals, both professional and personal. Setting goals provides clarity, drive and focus. We believe in designing your own "fit". We want to help your succeed.

FAQ Related to HR, Payroll and Benefits - INSERT POD Name

1. Will I still have a job?

2. Will my compensation change?

3. Will my benefits change? (consider all benefits, perks, and privileges)

4. Who will I report to?

5. Will I have to relocate?

6. Will I still have the same teammates?

7. Will my title or job responsibilities change?

8. Will our culture change?

9. Will our work processes change?

10. Will there be a severance package if I lose my job?

11. Will employees with previous years of service at [COMPANY] get credit for those years in their benefits once the merger takes place?

12. How will the merger impact the pension plan and retirement benefits?

13. Will a voluntary exit program be offered to employees? If so, what will be the minimum age?

14. What happens now that we have announced the merger?

15. Why did we decide that now was the right time to merge with [COMPANY]?

General

1. What happens now that we have announced the merger?

2. Why did we decide that now was the right time to merge with [COMPANY]?

General Employment

- When will I transition to [COMPANY]?

- Will I lose credit for my years of service with [COMPANY]

- Will I be in the same or a similar position after the transition?

- I work remotely today. Will I continue to work remotely after the transition?

- Is the [COMPANY] office moving?

Benefits & Compensation

- What happens the current benefits and compensation?

- What benefits does [COMPANY] offer?

- What will happen to my [COMPANY] 401(k)?

- Can I still use my Paid Time Off (PTO)?

FAQ: HR, Payroll and Benefits - FOR EMPLOYEES

Q1. When is pay day?

Pay day will be the 8th and 23rd of each month. In the event payday falls on a holiday or weekend, pay will be made available the business day prior. The first payroll will be XX.XX.XX. The pay periods are as follows

1. 16th thru the EOM: paid on the 8th

2. 1st thru the 15th: paid on the 23rd

Q2. Who do I contact for questions regarding payroll?

The Payroll Co. The _____ Team is here to assist you with all your payroll, benefits and HR questions. For your convenience, the team's contact information is below.

_____ Team

Email: _____

Phone: _____

Q3. How will these changes impact me? Will I still have a job? Who will I report to? Will my title or job responsibilities change? Will my compensation change?

This is a very exciting time for all of us and we understand that change can be concerning. We know each of you have many questions about how this change will impact you personally. As we complete the joining of our companies we will be answering all of your questions about your job, pay, benefits and many other operational questions that we know you all have. Please be patient as we complete this process. We appreciate your patience and look forward to answering all your questions very soon.

Q4. Will there be any advancement opportunities within the company?

Advancement opportunities will be considered based on employees' goals and the overall business needs of the organization

Q5. Where do I fit into the new organization?

Our Company has a culture of encouraging employees to set goals, both professional and personal. Setting goals provides clarity, drive and focus. We believe in designing your own "fit". We want to help your succeed.

Q6. Will our company policies and procedures be changing, such as vacation/sick time, holidays and other company benefits?

Not at this time; however, the current policies and procedures is being reviewed to ensure compliance with state and federal regulation. You will receive a copy of the final version once finalized.

Q7. Will we see a change in our benefits, such as health, dental and vision insurance? If so, when will these changes take place?

> There will be no change at this time to the benefits currently being offered. However, a review of available plans will be conducted and new plans will be considered. Should it be determined that a change will be made, the proper notice will be provided.

SHADOW SERVICES + LIGHT BULB CORP
= What does this mean for me?

General FAQ

This is a very exciting time for all of us and we understand that change can be confusing. We know each of you have many questions about how this change will impact you personally. As we complete the joining of our companies we will be answering all of your questions about your job, pay, benefits and many other operational questions that we know you all have. Please be patient as we complete this process. We appreciate your patience and look forward to answering all of your questions very soon.

This Company was founded many years ago and we are making steps to provide additional benefits to all members of the LIGHT BULB CORP Family and this is one of the ways we are thinking long term for each of your benefits.

Q1: Will the company name change?

> For now we will still operate under the LIGHT BULB CORP name as a subsidiary of the company name SHADOW SERVICES, Inc.

> We have and are discussing the potential of some point in the near future merging the names or creating an all together new name and brand for the industry, but for now we are not making any changes.

Q2: Will we see a change in our benefits? If so, when will these changes take place?

> There will be no change at this time to the benefits currently being offered. However, a review of available plans will be conducted and new plans will be considered. Should it be determined that a change will be made, the proper notice will be provided.

One of the most exciting parts of joining forces with our two companies is a thorough review of best practices which include everything from benefits to employees, discounts with vendors, as well as offerings available to our customers.

Q3: Will there be any change to my daily work?

For now there will be no change in your daily activities. We anticipate you working with your counterpart at SHADOW SERVICES to share ideas and best practices to help all levels improve.

Q4: Who should we call if we have any additional questions on concerns?

You will continue to report to your same supervisor until otherwise told.

Q5: Where do I fit into the new organization?

Our Company has a culture of encouraging employees to set goals, both professional and personal. Setting goals provides clarity, drive and focus. We believe in designing your own "fit". We want to help you succeed. We need you to succeed in order for us to succeed.

Q6: What type of additional resources will we now have available?

Additional resources are also available through the addition of _____ managers, _____ researchers, _____ engineers and additional reach in the industry. This will be through trade shows as well as in additional product offerings and collaboration.

Q7: When is pay day?

Pay day will not change. As you can imagine with a collaboration of companies at this level, there is a lot to work out. We are evaluating many different scenarios to streamline the processes;

however, we do not anticipate any changes to payroll dates before year end.

Q8: Will there be any advancement opportunities within the company?

Advancement opportunities will be considered based on employees' goals and the overall business needs of the organization. As we are now much larger, we should have more opportunities available for promotion within the Company.

Q9: Will our company policies and procedures be changing, such as vacation/sick time, holidays and other company benefits?

Not at this time; however, the current policies and procedures are being reviewed to ensure it is in align with our current offerings. You will receive a copy of the final version once finalized in the coming weeks.

Q10: Will we see a change in our benefits, such as health, dental and vision insurance? If so, when will these changes take place?

There should be no change at this time to the benefits currently being offered. However, a review of available plans will be conducted and new plans will be considered. Should it be determined that a change will be made, the proper notice will be provided.

Merger Transition Teams

Goal: Efficiently connect to acquired company personnel with a focus on identifying and retaining talent and synergies.

Team members should include at least 3-4 team members, ideally 1 person from each level of staff / managers / supervisor.

Upon the purchase of a new company 1-2 team members would fly out to the location with an owner partner and spend a few days in the new office.

1. Introductions would be made prior 24-48 hours prior to announcing the purchase, allowing team members to identify key players and potential problems.

2. Discussion with Owner and 'New LLC' Owner to determine any staff changes prior to announcement.

   a. This allows Owner presenting the Painted Picture vision to ensure everyone that their jobs are safe. Immediate reassurance will ensure high retention of talent.

   Staff will continue to work remotely for 24-48 hours.

3. This should provide a connection between the acquired firm and the WRIGLEY CORP Family.

Initial expense:

4. Cost of Flight and lodging.

Cost savings:

5. Cost of talent leaving due to uncertainty.

6. Cost of poor relationship and distrust.

Here is an example time line you can use. As mentioned elsewhere, if you search the Internet for "Acquisition strategy time line" you will get great examples. Regardless, you will want to tailor the time line to your organization. Additionally, you will want to assign each task an owner, by name, to be the responsible party for this portion of the project.

DUE DILIGENCE PROCESS: PRE-ACQUISITION PHASE

- 1 Company identified
- 2 Sign confidentiality agreement
- 3 Review and analyze: Market; Financial Statements; AR; customer lists; Leases and agreements
- 4 Start negotiations and prepare agreements
- 5 Obtain background check on owner(s) and staff (Similar to normal new hire process)
- 6 Determine employee needs - Identify potential strengths and admin positions that can be centralized.
- 7 Research company set-up requirements
- 8 Review IT network, security and integration and prepare recommendations
- 9 "Research licensing requirements" Moving into a new state, different registration, tax reporting created
- 10 Research HR, payroll and benefits requirements

DUE DILIGENCE PROCESS: PRE-SIGNING PHASE

- 1 Agreement: Draft
- 2 Operating Agreement: Draft

- 3 Assemble Integration Teams/ assign and integration manager. Team should consist of representatives of the company being acquired and the acquiring company. The team should discuss identified synergies and potential difficulties. — 3 weeks prior to announcement
- 4 Prepare time line of trigger dates. Use existing schedules and add dates — 3 weeks prior to announcement
- 5 "Identify potential points of Contact for ALL questions
- Email / Phone calls / Liaison or point of contact for ALL questions". Discuss confidentiality, peer to peer, admin and staff. Ensure match of staff to ensure needs are understood. — 3 weeks prior to announcement
- 6 Agreement: signed and fees paid
- 1a Prep Entity set-up and licensing LLC, DBA, Professional, City, State — 3 weeks prior to announcement
- 2a Prep Insurance: Liability and D&O — 4 weeks prior to announcement
- 3a "Prep Outplacement service agency" (Estimate on outplacement: $795 per person for a 3 month one-on-one placement service.) Split cost 50/50 (or all cost goes to acquired firm?) — 4 weeks prior to announcement
- 4a Prep Bank account
- 4b Letter to POD banker — Notify your bank of new entity in your consolidated company
- 5a Coordinate with Payroll Prep HR-payroll service agency — 4 weeks prior to announcement
- 6a Coordinate with Payroll Prep employee handbook — 2 weeks prior to announcement

- 7 Notify attorney and your CPA about expansion

PRELAUNCH: TRIGGER: SIGNED AGREEMENT AND RECEIPT OF FEES

•	1	Finalize Insurance: Liability and E&O	4 weeks prior to announcement
•	2	Finalize Entity set-up and licensing LLC, DBA, Professional, City, State	3 weeks prior to announcement
•	3	"Establish Point of Contact for ALL questions Email / Phone calls / Liaison or point of contact for ALL questions"	3 weeks prior to announcement
•	4	Coordinate with Payroll Arrange Prep HR-payroll service agency	4 weeks prior to announcement
•	5	Finalize Bank account: checks, stamps, etc	
•	6	Account debit paperwork	
•	7	Monthly billing	
•	8	Arrange Outplacement service agency	
•	9	Coordinate with Payroll	Distribute Prep employee handbook 2 weeks prior to announcement
•	10	"Prepare IT timeline related to computers Email, equipment, network, phones"	Be sure to plan for security upgrades for access to your system 3 weeks prior to announcement
•	11	Create a Question and answer email that will be checked by the integration manager.	Integration manager can route emails to others as necessary.
•	12	Insure logos and proper branding is in process	2 weeks prior to announcement

•	13	Prepare and book travel for owner and integration manager.	2 weeks prior to announcement
•	14	Plan training for announcement week	2 weeks prior to announcement
•	15	Draft press release	1 week prior to announcement
•	16	Draft announcements to employee and customers	1 week prior to announcement
•	17	Prep for distribution: FAQ: employees	
•	18	Prep for distribution: FAQ: contact sheet	
•	19	"FAQ: list of services"	
•	20	"Prepare Employee Welcome packet painted picture" "Welcome, now that you are a part of XYZ, here's what you can expect as an employee of XYZ" etc and we address a ton of these areas.	1 week prior to announcement
•	21	"Prepare Owner Welcome packet painted picture"	"Welcome, now that you are a part of XYZ, here's what you can expect as an employee of XYZ" etc and we address a ton of these areas. 1 week prior to announcement
•	22	Integration team	Arrive at office to identify synergies and problem areas. 1-2 days prior to announcement.

- 23 Integration manager

Discuss identified synergies and 'power' staff with owner. The POD will be staffed to their needs, meeting should identify sales or support staff that have the ability to retain or take customers. 1-2 days prior to announcement.

LAUNCH: ANNOUNCEMENT

- 1 Integration team Perform Trainings: Analytics, Materiality, Documentation.

  14 days before announcement

- 2 Admin Introduction - Announcement to New Employees

  "PowerPoint/Painted picture

- Communicate how things were done and how they will change (integrate huddle, explain dashboard)"
- 2 Distribute Owner Welcome packet
- 3 Distribute Employee Welcome packet
- 4 "Announcement to XYZ staff Internal announcement"

- 5   Admin Coordinate with Payroll

  "Employee Onboarding Distribute employee handbook" To ease transition all purchased companies should use the same XYZ handbook and have the same policies.

- 6   Distribute policies & procedures manual
- 7   Coordinate with Payroll For any outgoing staff, connect them with outplacement service.

  (Quote from outplacement firm: $795 per person for a 3 month one-on-one placement service.) Split cost 50/50 of all cost goes to acquired firm?

- 8   Insure all employees get independence / insider trading policy memo
- 9   (If relevant) Identify contact to distribute relevant information.
- 10   Admin Marketing

  Welcome letter customers (send)

- 11   Distribute press release
- 12   Tech

  Voicemail at POD changed

- 13   Integration team Perform Trainings on the XYZ way / systems

  Within 10 days after announcement

- 14   Admin/ social committee Coordinate with Payroll Gather Birthdays for birthday cards

- 15 Social Committee | Outreach- Skype introduction

ON-GOING

- 1 Integration Team Email/Phone calls/ Liaison or point of contact for ALL questions
  Daily for first week, then weekly for the first 6 months. These calls should focus on identifying any issues in the integration process. | Ongoing

- 2 Process training
  Majority of risk lies in lack of controls | First 3 months

- 3 Integration team
  Training with new retained staff on time entry procedures, work papers, etc... | Week 4 and beyond

- 4 Integration manager
  Follow-up Visits | Follow up visits twice in the first year to ensure the transition is moving along smoothly.

- 5 Social Committee
  Ongoing: Social committee informed of new contact for relevant events / parties / picnics | Ongoing

- 6 "Quarterly Quality Control checkup"
- 7 "Annual Quality Control inspection"
- 8 Schedule future milestones
- 9 Social Committee
  Identify 'Pen Pal' needs and make assignments. | Ongoing

- 10 Integration team
  Disbanded

After a first year or less the integration team should be 'Disbanded' to signify the completion or integration of the POD. At this point contact should not cease but should have been well established previous to dissolution of team that the dissolution is simply a symbolic formality.

Letter of Intent SHADOW NIGHTSTAND January 18, 2017 – this is just an example of one we have seen. We make no representations as to the binding or non-binding nature of the agreement and encourage you to seek legal counsel in preparation of your documents.

SHADOW SERVICES, Inc.
123 MAIN STREET
ANYTOWN USA

DATE

JOHN BRIAN / STEVEN FORD, Shareholders
NIGHT STAND SERVICES, Inc.
ANY OTHER TOWN, USA

Dear Messers. BRIAN AND FORD:

This letter ("Letter of Intent"), when agreed to and accepted by you for the purposes provided herein, shall evidence our respective intentions to proceed with negotiations, in good faith, with the objective of moving forward toward the execution of a definitive agreement (the "Common Stock Purchase Agreement") providing for the acquisition by SHADOW SERVICES INC. or its assignee (the "Purchaser") from 100% of the shareholders of NIGHT STAND SERVICES, Inc. (hereinafter referred to as the "Sellers") of all of the issued and outstanding capital stock of NIGHT STAND SERVICES, Inc. (collectively referred to herein as "NIGHT STAND") free and clear of all liens, claims and encumbrances, which is engaged in the business of equipment rentals, installations, services, and maintenance services.

It is understood that this Letter of Intent is not intended to constitute a binding agreement by and between Purchaser and Sellers to enter into the Common Stock Purchase Agreement, and no liability or obligation of any nature whatsoever is intended to be created hereunder, except as expressly set forth in this Letter of Intent. Purchaser and Sellers hereby agree to use their reasonable best efforts to negotiate, in good faith, the Common Stock Purchase Agreement as soon as practicable and within the time frame provided herein. This Letter of Intent does not contain all matters on which agreement must be reached in order to consummate the transactions contemplated herein, as it is intended solely as an outline of certain material terms.

The transactions contemplated in this Letter of Intent and the Common Stock Purchase Agreement are subject in all respects to the following terms and conditions:

1. Purchase of Stock by Purchaser; Purchase Price; Consideration.

    a. Purchaser shall acquire 100% of the issued and outstanding common stock of NIGHT STAND from Sellers (it being represented and warranted by Sellers by signing this letter that the capital stock of NIGHT STAND consists only of common stock) free and clear of all liens, claims and encumbrances. Adequate provisions for federal and state income taxes on taxable income through the date of Closing shall be estimated by NIGHT STAND, and sufficient cash shall be on hand at the date of Closing to pay such taxes. In addition to the amount estimated for federal and state income taxes as discussed above, there shall be sufficient cash and working capital on hand at Closing to allow NIGHT STAND to continue to operate in the ordinary course of business consistent with past practices without the injection of cash from the Purchaser. The amount of working capital to be on hand at the date of Closing shall be mutually agreed upon by the Sellers and Purchaser but in no event shall the amount of working capital on hand at closing be less than the amount of working capital as set forth on the NIGHT STAND balance sheet as of December 31, 2016 provided by Sellers to Purchaser (see Exhibit 1).

    b. Unless otherwise agreed to by both parties, the consideration shall be TWENTY-TWO MILLION FIVE HUNDRED THOUSAND Dollars ($22,500,000) plus certain assumed long-term debt set forth below to be paid and/or assumed in the following manner:

(i) ONE HUNDRED THOUSAND Dollars ($100,000) payable by cashier's check or by wire transfer at Closing;

(ii) ONE MILLION FIVE HUNDRED THOUSAND Dollars ($1,500,000) payable at Closing in common stock of Purchaser issued at a per share amount equal to the valuation amount of the Purchaser's common shares at December 31, 2016, which is estimated to be approximately FIVE percent (5%) of the then outstanding shares;

(iii) FOUR MILLION Dollars ($14,000,000), payable by a Seller Note ("Seller Note Number One"). Terms of the Seller Note Number One are: (a) TWO MILLION SIX HUNDRED SIXTY-SIX THOUSAND SIX HUNDRED SIXTY-SIX AND 66/100 Dollars ($2,666,666.66), payable by cashier's check or by wire transfer, at the conclusion of twenty four (24) consecutive months of Sellers' employment with Purchaser. In the event that either Seller terminates his employment prior to the 24 month employment contract, Sellers will forfeit all rights to the remaining unpaid balance of Seller Note Number One; and (b) ONE MILLION THREE HUNDRED THIRTY-THREE THOUSAND THREE HUNDRED THIRTY-THREE AND 34/100 Dollars ($1,333,333.34), payable by cashier's check or by wire transfer, at the conclusion of thirty six (36) consecutive months of Sellers employment with Purchaser. In the event that either Seller terminates his employment prior to the 36 month employment contract, Sellers will forfeit all rights to the remaining unpaid balance of Seller Note Number One. Additionally, at closing Sellers agree to deposit One Million Dollars cash or an equivalent amount of Purchaser common stock into an escrow account to be used as an inducement to retain certain of NIGHT STAND's key employees throughout the thirty six (36) consecutive months of Sellers' employment period. Seller Note Number One shall be callable at any time, at face value, by the Purchaser during the term of the note and will, at all times, be subordinate to the Purchaser's senior lenders. Seller Note Number One shall mature 36 months from the closing date, will accrue interest at the rate of 3% per annum and shall be convertible into the Purchaser's common stock at the Issue Share Price, at a time, and under terms and conditions, which are negotiated by the parties.

(iv) Purchaser shall assume, at Closing, certain bank and other long-term debt as set forth on Sellers' June 30, 2017 balance sheet, but in no event to exceed, $810,000 payable to Wells Fargo Bank (Note #7642234), $525,000 to Hibernia Bank (Note #5251064) and $150,000 to Wrigley Paws.

2. Purchase Price Adjustments.

a. Should sales from the NIGHTSTAND division be less than $15 Million for the year ended December 31, 2017, then the NIGHTSTAND Shareholders will return 1,000 shares of SHADOW stock (on a pro rata basis) to SHADOW for cancellation.

b. There shall also be a dollar for dollar purchase price net working capital adjustment to the Purchase Price based on the net working capital as of the date of the closing of the Transaction to the extent that the net working capital of NIGHTSTAND is not zero.

3. Consideration. In connection with the closing of the Transaction, the shareholders of NIGHTSTAND will receive total consideration of $10,000,000, plus options to purchase in the aggregate 100 shares of SHADOW common stock with an estimated value of $100,000 (the "Performance Options"). The Performance Option shall have a five year term, an exercise price of $10,000 per share, but shall only vest and become exercisable when NIGHTSTAND driven sales in any given year equal at least $15 million. The Purchase Price shall consist (1) 5,000 shares of restricted common stock in SHADOW (the "Initial

Shares") (with customary registration rights) issued at the closing with a $10,000 per share valuation, which is based upon an estimated 7x of owner adjusted EBITDA of projected $1,000,000 for 2018. and (2) a $5,000,000 promissory note (the "NIGHTSTAND Note"), bearing interest at the lowest applicable federal rate (which is 2.1% as of January 2017), and which is convertible at any time at the option of the holder of the NIGHTSTAND Note at a conversion rate of $10,000 per share, with the note being fully amortized using a 7 year schedule and payable monthly, with the balance of any principal and interest due on the fifth anniversary of the closing of the Transaction.

4. Put Right. In the event that valuation price of the SHADOW shares is not above $10,000 per share for during the first year after the closing of the Transaction, then (i) the NIGHTSTAND shareholders will have the option at any time during the 12 months after the first anniversary of the closing to force SHADOW to repurchase all or any part of their Initial Shares at a repurchase price of $10,000 per share, and (ii) the holder of the NIGHTSTAND Note shall have the option at any time after the first anniversary of the closing to force the Company to repurchase all or any part of the shares issuable upon conversion of the NIGHTSTAND Note at a repurchase price of $10,000 per share; provided however, if the holder of the NIGHTSTAND Note does not exercise the foregoing put right, the NIGHTSTAND Note will remain outstanding but at the election of the holder of the NIGHTSTAND Note, the Company shall issue an additional 1,000 shares of SHADOW shares to such holders in consideration for the cancellation of the foregoing put right related to the NIGHTSTAND Note.

In the event the NIGHTSTAND Shareholders or the holder of the NIGHTSTAND Note elects to exercise its put right above, the repurchase price may be paid over a five year period pursuant to a promissory note (the "Put Note") that bears interest at the lowest applicable federal rate, amortized over seven years and is payable in over the term of the Put Note on a pro rata basis with the NIGHTSTAND Note and the Exiting Notes (as defined below) to the extent of thirty (30%) percent of the EBITDA of SHADOW on a consolidated basis for such quarter. For purposes of this Letter of Intent, "EBITDA" is defined as Net Income determined in accordance with US generally accepted accounting principles on an accrual basis, after adding back the cost of Interest, Taxes, Depreciation and Amortization.

5. Employment Contracts; Non-Compete Agreements.

   a. At the date of Closing, certain key employees of NIGHT STAND shall enter into Employment Contracts with Purchaser for not more than a three (3) year period commencing upon the date of Closing, providing a salary and benefits (including employee stock options) comparable to other members of Purchaser's senior management in comparable positions. The terms and provisions of those Employment Contracts, and the salary, benefits and employee stock options, between Purchaser and key employees of NIGHT STAND shall be negotiated by Purchaser and Seller prior to Closing.

   b. These key employees shall also be required to execute a non-compete agreement in which they agree not to compete in a similar business of Purchaser. The term of the non-compete agreement shall be for a period of not less than two (2) years commencing upon the termination of their employment contract with Purchaser, and shall contain such other provisions as shall be mutually agreed upon prior to Closing.

6. Conditions. The Closing will be subject to the satisfaction of various conditions to be satisfied as of the date of Closing, which shall include, without limitation, the following:

   a. Common Stock Purchase Agreement. Purchaser and Sellers shall have negotiated, executed, and delivered a mutually satisfactory Common Stock Purchase Agreement and related documents which shall provide for the transactions contemplated hereby and include (without limitation): (i) representations and warranties of Purchaser and Sellers as are mutually acceptable and customary for

240

a transaction of the nature set forth herein; (ii) Closing conditions (including those specified herein) as are mutually acceptable; (iii) covenants pending prior to Closing and in effect thereafter (including those specified herein) as are mutually acceptable; (iv) indemnities as are mutually acceptable, including indemnities, if any, in favor of key NIGHT STAND employees which are at least as extensive as those which are currently in effect; and (v) forms of opinions of counsel as are mutually acceptable and customary for a transaction of the nature set forth herein.

b. Other Documents; Legal Opinions. Each other instrument contemplated by the Common Stock Purchase Agreement shall have been executed and delivered by each signatory hereto, and the opinions of counsel shall have been delivered.

c. Corporate and Shareholder Approvals. The Common Stock Purchase Agreement and the transactions contemplated thereby shall have been approved by the respective boards of directors of NIGHT STAND and Purchaser, the Purchaser's senior lenders and the shareholders of NIGHT STAND.

d. Consents and Approvals. All necessary government filings and approvals relating to the transactions contemplated by this Letter of Intent and the Common Stock Purchase Agreement, and all consents and approvals of third parties necessary for the consummation of the transactions contemplated by this Letter of Intent and the Common Stock Purchase Agreement, shall have been obtained.

e. Financial Statements. Prior to closing, Purchaser shall have received financial statements of NIGHT STAND for all of its prior fiscal years (since inception) and monthly financial statements of NIGHT STAND for the months subsequent to the end of the most recently completed fiscal year, which shall be satisfactory to Purchaser.

f. Due Diligence. Purchaser shall have conducted the legal, environmental, business, and financial due diligence reviews of NIGHT STAND (the "Due Diligence") it considers necessary, the results of which shall be materially consistent with Sellers' representations and warranties regarding such matters.

g. <u>Conditions Precedent.</u> The obligations of the parties to consummate the transactions contemplated by the Common Stock Purchase Agreement shall be subject to certain conditions precedent, including, without limitation, the following:

(i) The obligation of the Purchaser to perform in accordance with the Common Stock Purchase Agreement shall be subject to the completion of satisfactory financing arrangements required to provide the funding necessary to pay the cash portion of the consideration contemplated in Paragraph 1 herein. NIGHT STAND understands that Purchaser's lending sources may wish to conduct their own due diligence after September 1, 2017, and prior to closing.

(ii) The obligation of the Sellers to perform in accordance with the Common Stock Purchase Agreement shall be subject to the approval by Sellers, in its sole discretion, of the Private Placement Memorandum to be provided by Purchaser.

7. <u>Conditions.</u> The consummation of the Transaction shall be subject to satisfaction of the following conditions:

(a) the completion of a due diligence investigation by SHADOW of NIGHTSTAND's business, assets and liabilities, the scope and results of which shall be satisfactory to SHADOW in its sole discretion;

(b) the negotiation, execution and delivery of the Definitive Agreements, and the satisfaction or waiver of the conditions to closing set forth therein;

(c) satisfaction of all applicable federal and state filing and licensing requirements related to or in connection with the Transaction, and receipt of all applicable federal and state regulatory approvals required to consummate the Transaction;

(d) receipt of all third-party consents required to consummate the Transaction;

(e) the approval of the Transactions contemplated hereby by SHADOW's Board of Directors and NIGHTSTAND's Board of Directors and the shareholder approval of SHADOW to the extent required by law. SHADOW, Chambers and Marquez shall use their best efforts to obtain shareholder approval if so required.

(f) the completion of a due diligence investigation by NIGHTSTAND of SHADOW's business, assets and liabilities, the scope and results of which shall be satisfactory to NIGHTSTAND in its sole discretion.

(g) both parties to provide representations and warranties to the other in regards to the business; and

(h) concurrent with closing, existing debt holders of SHADOW, Chambers and Marquez agree to convert at least the greater of (a) fifty percent (50%) of the outstanding debt owed to them (the "Existing Debt") to equity in SHADOW and (b) such amount to reduce the Existing Debt payable to Chambers and Marquez to the same percentage of debt to equity being issued to the NIGHTSTAND shareholders in this Transaction. Chambers and Marquez also shall amend and restate their Existing Debt (x) to reduce the interest on such notes to the lowest applicable federal interest rate; (y) to modify the existing conversion price of such Existing Debt; and (z) to provide that such Existing Debt shall be paid on a quarterly basis pro rata with the NIGHTSTAND Note, and Put Note, if any, such that the quarterly payments on all such notes shall in the aggregate equal 35% of the EBITDA for of the consolidated SHADOW business for each quarter after the closing of the Transaction.

(i) the $1.0 million Frank Note shall be repaid in full with 90 days of the closing of the Transaction;

(j) SHADOW shall remove the personal guaranty of Williams on the NIGHTSTAND existing line of credit or on any obligations of NIGHTSTAND.

8. <u>Closing; Removal of Conditions on Purchaser's Obligation to Close.</u> The parties will negotiate in good faith with a view to executing the Common Stock Purchase Agreement on or before October 31,

2017. The Closing of the proposed transaction will take place as soon thereafter as all conditions to the transaction are satisfied or waived, but not later than December 31, 2017, unless an extension is mutually agreed upon. If the Common Stock Purchase Agreement is not executed by October 31, 2017, or such later date as the parties may agree, either party may terminate this Letter of Intent.

9. Closing; Subsequent Financing. The transaction is anticipated to close as soon as possible and the Parties commit to actively and diligently pursue completion no later than 30 days following the completion of this Letter of Intent.

10. Confidentiality. The parties agree that neither will use any of the information gathered pursuant to the proposed Due Diligence contemplated herein for any purpose other than the transaction anticipated by this Letter of Intent. Without the express written consent of all the parties hereto, each of the parties hereto agree to maintain in confidence and not disclose to any other person the existence of this Letter of Intent, the terms of the proposed transaction or the information delivered in connection with the proposed Due Diligence, other than disclosures required to obtain the approvals for the transaction contemplated hereby, disclosures to those professionals, advisors and potential financing sources and their attorneys who have a need to know, or any other disclosure required by applicable law. In the event that a party hereto is at any time requested or required (by oral questions, interrogatories, request for information or documents, subpoena or similar process) to disclose any information supplied to it in connection with this transaction to anyone other than professionals, advisors and potential financing sources and their attorneys, such party agrees to provide the other parties prompt notice of such request so that an appropriate protective order may be sought and/or such other parties may waive the first party's compliance with the terms of this paragraph. The parties acknowledge that their existing Confidentiality Agreement dated July 13, 2016, shall remain in full force and effect following the execution of this Letter of Intent.

11. <u>Conduct of Business.</u> Sellers agree that pending negotiation of the Common Stock Purchase Agreement, NIGHT STAND in all material aspects will operate its business only in the usual, regular and ordinary manner and in accordance with past practice so as to maintain the goodwill it now enjoys, and to the extent consistent with such operation, it will use all reasonable efforts to preserve its present officers and employees and to preserve relationships with customers and others having business dealings with it, including, but not limited to, paying suppliers and vendors in accordance with its usual business practices in a timely fashion.

o <u>Conduct of Business.</u> NIGHTSTAND will use its diligent efforts between the signing of the definitive documents and prior to the consummation of the transactions contemplated hereby to conduct its operations only in the ordinary course, to preserve its business organization intact and to preserve its goodwill and the confidentiality of its business know-how, to keep available to SHADOW the services of its present employees and to preserve for SHADOW the present relationships between NIGHTSTAND and its collaborators, licensors and others having business relations with NIGHTSTAND. Without limiting the generality of the foregoing and except as expressly set forth herein, NIGHTSTAND shall not, except in the ordinary course of business or except with the prior written consent of SHADOW, (i) sell any assets or sales of inventory in the ordinary course of business, (ii) incur any new indebtedness other than trade payables or other indebtedness incurred in the ordinary course of business, (iii) prepay or discharge any existing material indebtedness or material liabilities before normal due dates, (iv) alter or amend NIGHTSTAND's organizational documents, (v) issue or sell equity or rights to acquire equity of NIGHTSTAND, (vi) declare dividends on, make distributions with respect to, or redeem any portion of, the equity of NIGHTSTAND, (vii) materially increase the level of compensation or employee benefits of any employee, except in amounts in keeping with past practices by formulas or otherwise, or (viii) agree to do any of the foregoing. Notwithstanding anything to the contrary set forth above, SHADOW agrees that NIGHTSTAND shall be allowed to (a) enter into a new line of credit for NIGHTSTAND or term loan prior to the closing of the Transaction, (b) may repay the existing Alexander Loan of approximately $20,000, (c) may remove the existing personal guaranty of Alexander on any existing NIGHTSTAND obligation, and (d) NIGHTSTAND may pay a dividend or make any other cash distribution to its shareholders prior to the Transaction provided that such distribution does not result in a negative net working capital.

12. Exclusivity. NIGHT STAND and the Sellers shall immediately terminate negotiations and/or marketing efforts, if any, with others in regard to the sale of the stock of NIGHT STAND or the sale of NIGHT STAND's business and assets. Sellers shall not, prior to December 31, 2017, in the event the Common Stock Purchase Agreement is executed on or before October 31, 2017, solicit or initiate the submission of indications of interest, proposals, or offers from, or discuss or negotiate with any person relating to any direct or indirect acquisitions or purchase of any part of or all of the stock of NIGHT STAND, or any part of (other than an immaterial part of), or all of, the assets owned or to be owned by NIGHT STAND, nor will the Seller or NIGHT STAND discuss any merger, consolidation, or business combination with NIGHT STAND. Neither the Sellers nor NIGHT STAND shall furnish to any other person any information with respect to NIGHT STAND that could be used for the purposes described in this paragraph. Sellers shall promptly notify Purchaser of any acquisition proposal received by Sellers and shall provide Purchaser a copy (to the extent written) or description (to the extent made) of such acquisition proposal.

o Non-Solicitation or Negotiation With Others. In consideration of the execution of this Letter of Intent, NIGHTSTAND represents and agrees that, from the date hereof until the earlier of April 30, 2017 or the termination of this Letter of Intent in accordance with its terms, NIGHTSTAND shall discontinue all discussions or negotiations with other prospective purchasers of all or any substantial portion of NIGHTSTAND's business, assets or securities, and it will not, and will not permit any of its affiliates, officers, directors, employees, agents or representatives to, whether directly or indirectly, solicit or encourage (including by way of furnishing information) any inquiries or proposals relating to, or engage in any discussions or negotiations with respect to, the sale of all or any substantial portion of NIGHTSTAND's business, assets or securities, including any merger or consolidation, except for inquiries or proposals from, or discussions or negotiations with, SHADOW and its authorized representatives. NIGHTSTAND will promptly notify SHADOW of any such inquiry or proposal received by it, including information as to the identity of the parties involved and the specific material terms of any such inquiry or proposal.

13. Access. From the date of execution of this Letter of Intent, and until such time as the parties either terminate negotiations on the Common Stock Purchase Agreement or until the Closing, Sellers and NIGHT STAND shall cooperate with Purchaser in the performance by Purchaser of its Due Diligence. Upon execution of this Letter of Intent, and until such time as the parties either terminate negotiations on the Common Stock Purchase Agreement or until the Closing, Sellers and NIGHT STAND agree to grant to Purchaser and its authorized agents the right to inspect and audit the books and records of NIGHT STAND and to consult with those directors, officers, key employees, attorneys, auditors, and accountants of NIGHT STAND as Sellers shall approve upon request by Purchaser, such approval not to be unreasonably withheld, concerning customary due diligence matters. Such inspections and audits may include, for example, review and examination of NIGHT STAND's books and records of account, tax records, records of corporate proceedings, contracts, trademarks, governmental consents, and other business activities and matters relating to the transactions contemplated by this Letter of Intent and the Common Stock Purchase Agreement. All confidential information acquired by Purchaser pursuant to this

paragraph shall be held in the strictest of confidence by Purchaser and shall not be revealed or disclosed to any third party or parties, other than to Purchaser's professionals, advisors and potential funding sources and their attorneys, except as may be required by law. In the event the transaction should not be consummated for any reason after execution of the Common Stock Purchase Agreement, Purchaser shall promptly, upon request of NIGHT STAND, return all such documents as it may have obtained in this process, and any and all copies of such documents. The parties acknowledge that their existing Confidentiality Agreement dated July 13, 2016, shall remain in place following the execution of this Letter of Intent.

o   Information and Access; Confidentiality.

(a) NIGHTSTAND will afford to the officers, accountants, legal counsel and other representatives of SHADOW reasonable access to the properties, books, records and personnel of NIGHTSTAND in order that SHADOW may have full opportunity to make such investigation as it reasonably desires to make in connection with the transactions contemplated hereby.

(b) The parties acknowledge that SHADOW may obtain certain information about NIGHTSTAND, and that NIGHTSTAND may obtain certain information about SHADOW, which information is considered confidential and/or proprietary and which has not been otherwise made available to the public, including, without limitation, technical or marketing information, drawings, sketches, models, samples, computer programs, software, financial information, personnel or human resources information, and information related to business strategies, plans or projections, whether or not any of the foregoing is marked confidential, proprietary, private or restricted (the "Confidential Information"). Each party agrees not to (i) use such information for a purpose other than to evaluate the proposed transaction or (ii) except as required by law, disclose or disseminate the Confidential Information to any third party, except to its lawyers, accountants and others from whom such party seeks advice with respect to the

248

proposed transaction. Upon the written request of the other party, each party shall return to the other all Confidential Information and related materials or shall take all reasonable measures to ensure the destruction of such Confidential Information, and shall provide the other party with a written certification signed by an authorized officer that, to the best of his or her knowledge, after due inquiry, such return or destruction has occurred.

(c) <u>Public Announcements</u>. Except as may be required by law, none of the parties hereto shall engage in, encourage or support any publicity or disclosure of any kind or form in connection with this Letter of Intent or the transactions contemplated hereby or the existence of discussions or negotiations between the parties, whether to the financial community, governmental agencies or the public generally, unless the parties hereto mutually agree in advance on the form, timing and contents of any such publicity, announcement or disclosure.

14. <u>Costs and Expenses.</u> All costs and expenses incurred in connection with the negotiation, execution, and delivery of this Letter of Intent and the Common Stock Purchase Agreement and related agreements and the consummation of the transactions contemplated thereby shall be paid by the party incurring such costs and expenses, except that the Common Stock Purchase Agreement shall contain a provision that, in the event of a default under the Common Stock Purchase Agreement, the defaulting party shall pay the non-defaulting party's attorneys' fees incurred in connection with the negotiation, execution, and efforts toward consummation of the Common Stock Purchase Agreement. The costs and expenses incurred by the Purchaser shall include, but not be limited to, the costs and expenses of due diligence reviews and financial audits conducted at the Purchaser's request. Notwithstanding anything herein, the execution of this Letter of Intent does not obligate either party to enter into the Common Stock Purchase Agreement, but does obligate both to utilize their reasonable best efforts to negotiate the terms and provisions of such an Agreement in good faith.

a. Brokers' or Finders' Fees. Each party will indemnify and hold the other harmless from any claim for brokers' or finders' fees arising out of the transactions contemplated hereby by any person claiming to have been engaged by such party.

15. Termination. It is understood and agreed that if, despite the reasonable good faith efforts of the parties, a mutually satisfactory definitive Common Stock Purchase Agreement has not been executed on or before April 30, 2017, Purchaser and Seller may terminate this Letter of Intent by written notice to the other without any liability; provided, however, that the obligations set forth in paragraphs 4 and 6 through 13 shall survive.

16. Nature of Letter of Intent. The provisions of paragraphs 4 through 13 hereof are intended to be binding upon the parties in accordance with their terms. With respect to all other matters set forth herein, it is understood that: (i) this Letter of Intent sets forth the intentions of the parties to use their reasonable best efforts to negotiate, in good faith, a Common Stock Purchase Agreement and that any legal obligations with respect to such matters, including, but not limited to, the customary representations and warranties described in paragraph 3(a), shall be only as set forth in the Common Stock Purchase Agreement when and if executed by Purchaser and Sellers, and (ii) that neither Purchaser (or any affiliate thereof) nor Sellers shall be responsible for any claims or liability relating to the transactions contemplated hereby in the event the Common Stock Purchase Agreement is not so executed and delivered, except as expressly provided in the Letter of Intent.

17. Indemnification. The Sellers represent and warrant that the Purchaser will not incur any liability of any kind or nature whatsoever in connection with the consummation of the acquisition of NIGHT STAND to any third party with whom the Seller or its agents have had discussions regarding the disposition of NIGHT STAND, and the Sellers agree to indemnify, defend and hold harmless the Purchaser, its officers, directors, stockholders, lenders and affiliates from any

claims by or liabilities to such third parties, including any legal or other expenses incurred in connection with the defense of such claims.

18. <u>Governing Law.</u> This Letter of Intent shall be governed by and construed in accordance with the laws of the State of Louisiana, without giving effect to principles of conflicts of laws.

19. <u>Miscellaneous.</u> This Letter of Intent constitutes the complete understanding of the parties with respect to the matters referenced herein, and any other agreements, contracts or understanding (whether written or oral) are superseded by the terms hereof. The rights and obligations of the parties created by this Letter of Intent shall not be assignable by either party without the prior written consent of the other party, which will not be unreasonably withheld. Notwithstanding the foregoing, the rights and obligations of Purchaser created by this Letter of Intent shall be assignable by Purchaser without the prior written consent of Seller only to the ultimate holding company contemplated by this agreement. This Letter of Intent may be signed in one or more counterparts, each of which taken together shall constitute one and the same agreement.

- <u>Intent of the Parties.</u> It is understood and agreed that this Letter of Intent, when executed by all of the parties hereto, constitutes a statement of mutual intentions with respect to the proposed transaction, but does not contain all matters upon which agreement must be reached in order for the proposed transaction to be consummated and a commitment with respect to the proposed transaction will result from the execution of the Merger Agreement, subject to the terms and conditions expressed therein. Notwithstanding the two preceding sentences of this Section 15, the provisions of Sections 8, 9, and 11 through 18 are agreed to be fully binding on the parties hereto upon the execution of this Letter of Intent. The provisions of Sections 8, 9 and 12 through 16 shall survive the termination of this Letter of Intent.

If the terms of this Letter of Intent are acceptable to you, please sign and return a counterpart to the undersigned.

Very truly yours,

SHADOW SERVICES, Inc.

By: _____
                   Abigail Paige, CEO

_____
                 NAME

_____
                 NAME

Agreed to and accepted as of the date first above written:

NIGHT STAND SERVICES, Inc.

By: _____
            JOHN BRIAN, Shareholder

Exhibit A

Capitalization Table of SHADOW SERVICES, Inc.

(attached hereto)

YOUR LOGO HERE

POD AGREEMENT

XYZ, LLC and Seller John

THIS AGREEMENT made and entered into effective as of the day of, by and between XYZ, LLC. ("XYZ, LLC"), a limited liability company organized and existing under the laws of the State of Nevada, with a principal place of business at _____Drive, Las Vegas, NV 89____ and JOHN, an individual, an Arizona resident. This is a non-binding term sheet and a formal legal agreement will be drafted upon your acceptance of these terms.

Whereas, XYZ, LLC, is a Nevada LLC and is a _____ (type of product or service) firm, and seeks to start a new company focused on Consulting services in _____ (location), known hereinafter as the "New XYZ Company", and have them operate under the XYZ, LLC brand. Collectively, ""XYZ, LLC" and the New XYZ Company is hereinafter known as "the parties".

1. XYZ, LLC will contribute the fees for the formation and registration of the new LLC, to operate as summarized below. Those fees will be reimbursed by the new entity within ninety (90) days.

2. A new LLC will be formed, hereinafter known as the "new LLC", by XYZ, LLC, in the State of Nevada, the capital ownership of which will be 50% JOHN, and 50% XYZ, LLC.

3. The legal name of the new LLC will be XYZ Arizona 1, LLC. However, the company will operate under the name "XYZ, LLC", while making every attempt to comply with the DBA provisions.

4. A business checking account will be opened under the name of the new LLC.

5. XYZ, LLC will coordinate the Human Resources, Payroll and Benefits and the routine processing of all functions for the new LLC

6. XYZ, LLC will coordinate all other normal practice administration procedures as required to assist in operating the Practice of the New XYZ Company.

7. XYZ, LLC will provide the Information Technology (IT) support, hardware, and equipment needs.

8. XYZ, LLC will be responsible for coordinating, reviewing, and implementation of software to include, accounting, CRM, database, or otherwise.

9. XYZ, LLC management to approve of acceptance of new customers and purchases.

10. All costs directly related to the "new LLC" such as Rent, Payroll and Business Insurance shall be absorbed by the ""new LLC".

11. MANAGEMENT FEE: The "new LLC" shall pay XYZ, LLC a Management Fee of 6% of Gross Collections on a monthly basis. This fee will be automatically deducted from the new LLC bank account via ACH.

12. PROFIT ALLOCATION: The allocation of net Profits of the "new LLC" shall be 50% JOHN and 50% XYZ, LLC.

13. LOSS ALLOCATION: In the unlikely event the "new LLC" incurs operating losses they shall be absorbed 50% by XYZ, LLC and 50% by JOHN.

14. GUARANTEED PAYMENTS: Prior to the execution of this Agreement the parties may agree to a schedule Guaranteed Payments for the proprietor of the "New XYZ Company" as consideration prior to the 50/50 Profit Allocation in Number 12 above. – **(this may adjust based on how you intend on them taking a salary)**

15. XYZ, LLC PROFESSIONAL LABOR: In the event the "new LLC" wishes to use the XYZ, LLC professional labor pool the "new LLC" will be charged 125% of the base salary of the professional labor used for that particular customer, and be measured in terms of hours spent on the project.

16. BUSINESS DEVELOPMENT BONUS: In the event the "new LLC" brings in other acquisitions or POD candidates, and said acquisitions are accepted and completed by XYZ, LLC, the proprietor of the "New XYZ Company" will receive a ___% bonus of the amounts collected by XYZ, LLC respective to this acquisition for a period of three (3) years from the date of the acquisition.

17. RIGHT OF FIRST REFUSAL: XYZ, LLC shall retain a Right of First Refusal to purchase the Client List of the "New XYZ Company", at any time during the life of the "new LLC", at a price of 70% of the twelve months of gross collections immediately preceding the date of this Agreement.

18. PURCHASE RIGHTS: XYZ, LLC has the right to purchase, the day after the fifth anniversary date of this Agreement, the remaining 50% of the "new LLC" from its owner. The purchase price of the Client List for the remaining 50% capital ownership interest in the "new LLC" shall be determined at a rate of 90% of the twelve months of gross collections immediately preceding the date of this agreement, and shall be paid in three equal annual increments, initially on the purchase date, and then the first and second annual anniversary dates of which XYZ, LLC exercised its purchase rights.

19. DISSOLUTION: The "new LLC" may be dissolved within the first year by a thirty day notice by either party. After the first anniversary date of this Agreement if the XYZ, LLC desires to dissolve the "new LLC", XYZ, LLC has the right to buy the remaining 50% of the LLC under the terms set-out in Number 13 of this Agreement, irrespective of the fifth anniversary date provision.

20. GOODWILL BONUS: In the likely event that the "new LLC" grows its Customer List (from the customers on Exhibit A attached) while operating under the XYZ, LLC brand the Seller shall be entitled to a bonus relating to the increase in the Customer List that increased under the "new LLC". The bonus shall be computed as __% of the amounts collected from Gross Billings of the Client List on the date XYZ, LLC exercises its purchase rights over the amount of collections from Gross Billings as of the date of this Agreement, and payable in three annual increments in accordance with the dates set-forth in Number 13 above.

21. LEGAL JURISDICTION: The legal jurisdiction for arbitration or litigation shall be in the county where the "new LLC" is located, which in this case is Arizona.

Agreed to:

By: _____

       SELLER JOHN Date Title

Acknowledged:

_____

XYZ, LLC   Date

ABOUT THE AUTHOR

Jason F. Griffith, CPA, CMA, is the founder of Yes If…, a strategy and acquisition consulting firm in Las Vegas. He is a licensed Certified Public Accountant and Certified Management Accountant and earned a master's degree in accounting from Rhodes College in Memphis, Tennessee. He lives in Las Vegas with his wife and children. He can be found at @jasonfgriffith on Twitter and at www.YesIf.com.